Toronto
Public
Library

Human rights violations against the indigenous peoples of the Americas

Toronto
Public
Library

Al Index: AMR 01/08/92

ISBN 0-939994-80-1

First Published: October 1992

Amnesty International USA
322 Eighth Avenue
New York, NY 10001

Printed by:
  John D. Lucas Printing Co.

Copyright:
  Amnesty International
  Publications

Original language: English

CONTENTS

INTRODUCTION

Throughout history groups have dominated and colonized others, often at great cost to the subjugated culture. The region now called the Americas has been no exception. Before the arrival of Europeans, vast areas of the Americas were ruled by Indian empires, such as the Aztecas and the Toltecs, whose subjects risked enslavement and execution. Since colonization, indigenous peoples in the Americas have suffered gross and widespread human rights violations, including extrajudicial executions. Combined with the ravages of disease and starvation, these abuses have decimated and, in some cases, eliminated indigenous populations in the Americas. There is no longer an indigenous community on Hispaniola, the island where Columbus landed during his first visit to the "New World" and where many of the official ceremonies will be held in October 1992 to mark the quincentenary of his arrival in the Americas.

Mass killings of indigenous peoples may have reduced in scale over the past 500 years, but they have never stopped. Scholars agree that Indians were a particular target when the army broke the peasant revolt in El Salvador in 1932. Some 30,000 people are believed to have been killed, many of them indigenous. The great majority of the Indians who survived abandoned their communities and traditional dress to avoid summary execution, and from then on no longer spoke indigenous languages in public. The counter-insurgency tactics the Guatemalan army pursued to crush the armed opposition in the late 1970s and early 1980s claimed tens of thousands of non-combatant Indian peasants among its victims. Many of those who fled sought anonymity in the cities, abandoning the traditional clothing that would have identified them not only as indigenous, but also as natives of areas considered "subversive" by the authorities.

Throughout the Americas members of national security forces, either in uniform or in the guise of "death squads", and their civilian auxiliaries continue to be responsible for gross and widespread human rights violations against indigenous peoples. They are not the sole perpetrators. In several countries in the region private agents — hired gunmen, civilian vigilantes, armed groups of settlers, drug traffickers — are responsible for persistent abuses such as the abduction and murder of Indians. These otherwise common crimes become human rights violations when they are committed with official collusion or acquiescence, for example, when the state consistently fails to investigate them or to bring those responsible to justice. In countries racked by civil conflict members of armed opposition groups have also attacked indigenous people, often when they refused to take sides in the armed conflict between opposition groups and the government. Some of the most vulnerable indigenous groups are also the most isolated.

The circumstances in which indigenous peoples fall victim to human rights violations vary widely across the Americas. In Mexico and Ecuador, Indians involved in bitter struggles for land have been routinely arrested and tortured, and some have been extrajudicially executed. Native Americans in the USA await judicial execution in the horror of death row. In some countries Indians are living in a state of siege. The indigenous communities of Peru, caught in a decade of conflict between government forces and armed opposition groups, have suffered abduction, torture and killing on a mass scale.

Activists for indigenous rights throughout the Americas have paid for their commitment with their lives and liberty. Indigenous peoples have been victimized because they spoke out against the abuses suffered by their communities, or because they were active in groups protesting against those abuses. Others have been singled out because of their involvement in trade union or political organizations.

Sometimes abuses result from government actions directed at people of particular ethnic origin. In parts of the Americas, discrimination has forced indigenous peoples to the margins of society. In many contexts evangelization or assimilation has weakened their cultural identity. Indigenous peoples are often economically disadvantaged and marginalized from the societies in which they live by geographical, cultural and linguistic factors. Discrimination often renders them more vulnerable to abuse than other sectors of society. They may be more likely to be prosecuted or convicted for certain offences than people from other racial groups and may have limited or no access to adequate legal representation. In some countries, they are apparently also more likely to suffer harsher penalties than non-indigenous people convicted of similar crimes. In a number of countries, indigenous prisoners

Killings on a massive scale, as well as disease and starvation, have decimated the indigenous populations of some countries in the Americas. It is estimated that there are now some one-and-a-half million Native Americans in the USA. Some sources suggest that when Europeans first arrived, the USA's indigenous population may have exceeded 12 million. In Brazil, the population at the time of colonization is believed to have been five million; today it is officially estimated at 220,000.© Julio Etchart

allege that they are more likely to be ill-treated while in custody.

In theory, indigenous peoples in the Americas are protected against human rights violations by provisions in both national and international law. However, the degree to which protective legislation is enforced falls short of its potential. This is illustrated in country after country, in cases which range from direct involvement by state agents in human rights violations through to a general failure to protect indigenous peoples against abuses. Only rarely are the perpetrators brought to justice.

Amnesty International's primary emphasis is on governments because of their special responsibility under international law to respect human rights. However, the organization also unequivocally opposes and condemns deliberate and arbitrary killings, torture and hostage-taking by armed opposition groups. Deliberate and arbitrary killings include intentional killings of civilians, prisoners and others taking no part in hostilities. In Peru, for example, where indigenous people have repeatedly been victimized by both sides to the civil conflict, Amnesty International calls on both the government and the armed opposition to respect fundamental humanitarian standards.

Despite a 500-year legacy of abuse, throughout the centuries indigenous peoples in the Americas have struggled to preserve their cultures, their identities, and often their lives. Currently, there is a resurgence of indigenous organization, and groups throughout the region are working at community, national, regional and international level to ensure the protection of their civil, political, economic, social and cultural rights, and to bring their demands to public attention. As a result, some governments in the Americas, as well as intergovernmental bodies, are devoting increased attention to indigenous questions. Concern for indigenous affairs in the Americas has spread beyond the region. The United Nations (UN) Sub-Commission's Working Group on Indigenous Populations has met annually since 1982 to review developments which affect the rights of indigenous peoples and to develop standards concerning indigenous rights. The European Parliament, noting "reports from Amnesty International and Survival International of human rights violations against indigenous peoples", has instructed its human rights unit to appoint a rapporteur to "analyze the human, territorial and cultural rights of the indigenous peoples of the Americas".

Meanwhile, a growing international awareness of environmental and ecological issues coincides in some cases with indigenous peoples' traditional beliefs and practices concerning the protection of the environment, and has gained some indigenous organizations new allies on the national and international level. This has helped focus attention on the abuses which indigenous peoples suffer and the efforts they are making to protect their lives, their cultures, and their lands and resources.

Amnesty International and indigenous rights

Amnesty International has campaigned against the human rights violations suffered by indigenous people all over the world. The organization has, for example, repeatedly called for inquiries into killings of tribal people in the Chittagong Hill Tracts of Bangladesh by members of the security forces, including the Village Defence Party, a civilian defence force with official status. Amnesty International has repeatedly called for action against human rights violations inflicted on non-combatant indigenous people in Myanmar by government forces on counter-insurgency duty. In February 1992 the organization launched a campaign against political killings in the Philippines, where several members of tribal communities in the Cordillera region

Native Americans march for "Mother Earth". Growing international concern for the environment often coincides with traditional indigenous practices and has gained indigenous peoples new allies on the international level.
©*Julio Etchart*

were killed in circumstances strongly suggesting official involvement. They were apparently singled out because of their work for tribal peoples' rights. In March 1992 Amnesty International launched a worldwide campaign against torture, rape, and death in custody in India, where many of the victims were tribal people. In Australia, where there is a high incidence of Aboriginal deaths in custody, Amnesty International has called on the government to fully investigate these deaths and to bring to justice any officials implicated in abuses.

For many years, Amnesty International has campaigned against the abuses suffered by indigenous peoples in the Americas. However, the organization considers that 1992, the 500th anniversary of the arrival of Europeans in the Americas, is an appropriate time to focus special attention on human rights issues affecting indigenous peoples, and those working with them, in that region. It has therefore initiated a special program of activities, "500 years on", to highlight the human rights violations — including extrajudicial executions, "disappearances", arbitrary arrests, torture and ill-treatment, unfair trials of political prisoners and the judicial death penalty — suffered by indigenous peoples in the Americas.

In the context of this program of activities and in line with its normal policy of responding to specific reports of human rights violations, Amnesty International has produced a series of special actions on abuses perpetrated against specific groups, such as the Mapuche of Chile, the Ticuna, Atikum and Truka of Brazil, and the Mixe, Zapotec, Ch'ol and Tzeltal of Mexico. In the first five months of 1992 the organization initiated 14 Urgent Action appeals on behalf of 78 indigenous people in the Americas whom it considered in imminent danger of suffering abuses such as torture, "disappearance" or extrajudicial execution.

In preparation for its "500 years on" campaign, Amnesty International has recently visited Brazil, Mexico, the USA and Canada, to research human rights violations against indigenous peoples. Other visits, to Panama, Bolivia and Argentina, for example, have included contacts with indigenous organizations among their objectives. Amnesty International also followed the deliberations of the UN Working Group on Indigenous Populations with special interest at both its 1991 and 1992 sessions in Geneva in order to develop closer contacts with indigenous organizations. The organization also sent a delegation to the meeting held in Guatemala in October 1991 when indigenous organizations from throughout the

The Chilean Section of Amnesty International recently produced a copy of the Universal Declaration of Human Rights in the Mapuche language.

A Peruvian woman reads Amnesty International's 1985 Briefing on Peru.

Americas met to plan activities in 1992 to call attention to the plight of indigenous peoples in the region. In March 1992 Amnesty International representatives attended a conference in Caracas, Venezuela, which focused on women in the context of the 500th anniversary.

As part of its ongoing efforts to arouse international concern regarding human rights violations within its mandate directed against indigenous peoples and others in the Americas, Amnesty International has also taken its concerns directly to intergovernmental organizations, including the UN, the International Labour Organisation (ILO), and the Organization of American States (OAS).

In a submission to the UN Sub-Commission on Prevention of Discrimination and Protection of Minorities in 1983, Amnesty International noted that certain of the rights sought by indigenous peoples, such as self-determination and the right to preserve indigenous culture, tradition, language and way of life, did not fall within the organization's mandate, but that it was often in the context of indigenous peoples' efforts to win recognition and enjoyment of these rights that Amnesty International acted to prevent or respond to cases of arbitrary detention, unfair trial, torture, "disappearance" or extrajudicial execution. Amnesty International's submissions to the Inter-American Commission on Human Rights (IACHR) of the OAS have repeatedly drawn attention to abuses against indigenous peoples of the Americas. In 1979, for example, Amnesty International testified to the IACHR about abuses in Guatemala, including the killing in May 1978 of over 100 Kekchí Indians, including women and children shot down without warning by government troops after they had gone to the town of Panzós, Alta Verapaz, to discuss an official letter they had recently received regarding a land dispute.

This report does not survey all abuses of indigenous peoples' human rights; it focuses on those rights which fall within Amnesty International's strictly defined mandate. Amnesty International covers a limited spectrum of fundamental rights, but not because it ignores the importance of others. Although there is a close relationship between all human rights, Amnesty International believes that it can achieve more by working within set limits. However, it recognizes the vital importance of upholding other rights, including the economic, social and cultural rights protected in the Universal Declaration of Human Rights, and campaigns for governments to ratify the International Covenant on Economic,

Social and Cultural Rights as well as the International Covenant on Civil and Political Rights (ICCPR).

This report is not an exhaustive account of Amnesty International's work on behalf of indigenous peoples. Nor does it describe all the abuses that indigenous peoples have suffered, or the initiatives they have taken to attain their objectives and protect their rights. It is intended as a survey of the type, context and pattern of human rights violations within Amnesty International's mandate against indigenous peoples in recent years. Certain issues, countries or indigenous groups whose members have been among the victims may not be reflected here for reasons such as lack of access to information and the difficulties of research in remote areas, and the fact that in some countries indigenous people have been decimated or virtually eliminated by large-scale abuses carried out during or after the original colonization.

In the early 1980s, at the height of the army counter-insurgency campaign which claimed the lives of tens of thousands of non-combatant Indians in Guatemala, a leader of a Guatemalan indigenous peasant organization had this to say about the work of international human rights organizations:

> "*Your work has supported and renewed our conviction that no matter how poor or ill-treated we are, we have the right to life and to respect, that to kill a new-born baby or an old person bowed down by the persecution of the army constitutes a ... crime that deserves the most energetic condemnation.*
>
> "*I believe that it is on this point that [your] work and our own as a peasant organization converge: the defence of the right to life in all its aspects: the right to physical integrity, to security ... to a simple but fully human life, the end to all of the threats that have weighed so heavily on our people, both Indian and ladino[1] for so many centuries.*"

1

The abuses indigenous peoples suffer

Amnesty International recognizes the importance of all abuses of human rights. However, its work focuses on preventing certain violations of fundamental rights: extrajudicial execution and the judicial death penalty, "disappearance", torture and ill-treatment, imprisonment of prisoners of conscience, and unfair trial for political prisoners.

A wide range of human rights violations is suffered by indigenous peoples in the Americas. Often, these violations are interconnected. Arbitrary arrest may be followed by torture. Under torture a "confession" may be extracted, often in a language the detainee does not speak or read. This "confession" may then be used to unfairly convict the victim when he or she is brought to trial. The trial may be conducted in a language which the defendant does not speak or in which he or she is not fluent.

Although the types of abuse suffered by indigenous peoples are not unique to them, they may often suffer such violations solely because of their racial origin. Economically disadvantaged and marginalized by geographical, cultural and linguistic factors, they often have little access to state institutions through which to seek redress. Ignorance of the language of the dominant society, and of its social and legal customs and judicial system, which are often in conflict with their traditional practices, makes it more difficult for them to seek redress when their rights are violated. Discrimination and limitations, which in some countries are placed on their civil and political rights, are further factors which can limit indigenous peoples' access to means of redress.

'The homicidal state'

"The great mass murderers of our time have accounted for no more than a few hundred victims. In contrast, states that have chosen to murder their own citizens can usually count their victims by the carload lot. As for motive, the state has no peers, for it will kill its victim for a careless word, a fleeting thought, or even a poem.

"But the homicidal state shares one trait with the solitary killer—like all murderers, it trips on its own egotism and drops a trail of clues which, when properly collected, preserved and analyzed are as damning as a signed confession left in the grave."

Dr Clyde Snow, forensic anthropologist, who has applied his skills in the scientific disinterment and analysis of skeletal remains to expose atrocities committed by state agents in a number of countries including Argentina, Bolivia, Chile and Guatemala.

Extrajudicial execution

Extrajudicial executions are officially sanctioned killings without any legal or judicial process. In some situations of civil conflict, a policy of mass extrajudicial executions has been employed against individuals and entire communities suspected of supporting government opponents, or to remove potential sources of logistical support for the armed opposition.

The tales of the destruction of entire villages and the extrajudicial execution of thousands of indigenous peasants which began to emerge as civil war ravaged Guatemala in the early 1980s were so horrific that they strained credulity. The Guatemalan military was carrying out a counter-insurgency program that relied on the mass murder of non-combatant civilians. In July 1982, 302 people were slaughtered by Guatemalan soldiers at the San Francisco estate, Nentón, in a largely Chuj-speaking area of Huehuetenango. At first the government denied the massacre had occurred. However, many of the survivors fled to Mexico, and gave accounts of the massacre to priests working in the refugee camps. The priests matched the refugees' testimonies with accounts collected from witnesses who had stayed in Guatemala. Villagers told how men, women and children were shot, stabbed, beheaded, hacked to death with machetes, disembowelled and burned alive. The priests recorded the names of all of those who had died; 91 were children under the age of 12; the

11

youngest victim, André Paíz García, was a baby of two months.

Thousands of people reported "disappeared" during the civil war in Guatemala, particularly indigenous peasants, had in fact been killed by the army and buried in secret graves. Knowledge of the location of the clandestine burial sites seems to be widespread in Guatemala. Efforts to locate missing relatives by checking "body dumps" are so common that when Amnesty International delegates, visiting Guatemala in 1988, asked a peasant for directions to a clandestine burial site, he replied, "Oh, are you looking for relatives?" and gave directions to the nearest site. Despite widespread knowledge as to where the clandestine cemeteries are located, the authorities are not known to have initiated any efforts to investigate them. The few exhumations to have taken place occurred only after repeated pressure from relatives and local human rights groups.

In individual cases of extrajudicial execution, sufficient evidence sometimes exists to establish how those buried in clandestine graves were murdered and who was responsible. In Guatemala, forensic analysis of remains has recently been used to confirm identities and support testimonial evidence regarding the cause and manner of death of indigenous victims of extrajudicial executions.

In November 1990 Manuel Cos Morales, a Quiché Indian, filed a complaint with the regional human rights ombudsman in Santa Cruz del Quiché against a member of the civil patrol in his village, San Antonio Sinaché. According to Cos Morales, the man had been responsible for the 1984 slaying of his brother and three other Quiché Indians. A forensic delegation organized by Physicians for Human Rights and Americas Watch, visiting Guatemala in 1990, travelled to the site of the grave and supervised the exhumation of the four victims. Some of the villagers were able to give eye-witness accounts of the killings. One of the victims, 35-year-old Manuel Tiniguar Chitic, was apparently killed for missing civil patrol duty because he was away from the village working in sugar cane fields on the Pacific Coast. According to the villagers, his hands were bound behind his back, he was tied to a tree, and beaten with machetes and sticks. When he collapsed, he was thrown into a hastily dug grave in a nearby banana grove. Forensic analysis established that the remains were those of a right-handed American Indian male, approximately five-and-a-half feet tall and 35 years old, characteristics which matched Manuel Tiniguar Chitic. The rope used to bind the victim's hands behind his back was still tied around the tattered remnants of his sleeves. The other bodies were also exhumed and identified; the forensic findings as to the manner of their deaths also coincided with eye-witness accounts. However, despite the case thus built as to how the San Antonio Sinaché peasants died, Amnesty International knows of no proceedings initiated against those allegedly responsible.

During the 12-year civil war which racked El Salvador, the army carried out human rights violations on a massive scale against members of civilian grass root organizations which they regarded as a source of support for the armed opposition group, the Farabundo Martí National Liberation Front (FMLN). One of the organizations repeatedly characterised as "subversive" by the authorities is the Salvadorian National Indigenous Organization (ANIS). It was formed in 1954 to defend the rights of Salvador's remaining indigenous peoples. On a number of occasions, abuses against ANIS members have been reported. In 1983 the Salvadorian army was responsible for the so-called Las Hojas massacre, which occurred when more than 200 soldiers raided two small Indian farming cooperatives in the west of the country. Dozens of unarmed Indian peasants, some of them ANIS members, were extrajudicially executed. The army attacked after a local landowner, reportedly angry because the cooperative would not permit him to build a road through its land, denounced the cooperativists to the military authorities as "subversives", with fatal results for the Indians.

ANIS members have continued to suffer abuses which, in many cases, appear to have been linked to their advocacy of indigenous rights. In March 1990 Efraín Cabrera Quintanilla and his wife Cristina Alvarez de Cabrera were shot dead in their home in Ahuachapán, by soldiers from a nearby military base. Both were members of ANIS. On the same day Samuel Pérez Jérez, also an ANIS member, was shot dead in Ahuachapán by a man in civilian clothes.

Over the past nine years — between January 1983 and May 1992 — Amnesty International has documented the cases of at least 4,200 people who "disappeared" in Peru after being detained by the security forces. Many of the victims were indigenous. By the end of May 1992 the vast majority of these remained unaccounted for. Thousands more appear to have been killed since 1983 by government forces in extrajudicial executions, including some 500 people in 18 separate massacres documented by Amnesty International.

In August and September 1990 soldiers and members of a civil defence group reportedly extrajudicially executed villagers from

In the plaza of Huamanga
The bombs are exploding
In the city of Huamanga
The bullets are raining down
The innocents are crying in
the prisons
And the neighbourhoods of
Huamanga
Are crying tears of blood
The blood of the hills, by
Carlos Falconi

various small communities in Huanta and Huamanga provinces, department of Ayacucho, because they had refused to participate in patrols after attacks in the area by the armed opposition. Some 34 people, including children, are believed to have been killed and others were detained. A journalist described the scene when the bodies of some of the victims were exhumed from mass graves at a ravine called Chilcahuaycco: "... the relatives find a second grave ... After removing the branches, cactus and stones, everyone starts digging frantically, some with spades, others with pickaxes, and others with their bare hands. Nearly all of them are crying and the stench is increasing. The first big bone appears, long, like a huge accusing finger. The weeping of the relatives turns to melancholy songs in the local Quechua dialect. Zacarías Cconocc Huayhua ... sings words of grief to his wife whom he has just recognized".

A Peruvian Senate commission established in 1990 to investigate gross human rights violations found that the killings at Chilcahuaycco had been committed by members of the army and a civil defence patrol. In February 1992 it was reported that a lower civilian court had found sufficient evidence to charge one officer with aggravated homicide in connection with the Chilca-huaycco killings.

Extrajudicial executions of indigenous peoples in the Americas have also been carried out by "death squads" composed of police officers and soldiers in plain clothes, by civilian auxiliaries under military command, and by privately hired gunmen whose activities are officially supported or condoned.

Opposition forces have also been responsible for individual and mass killings, often directed at those who refuse to support them. On 13 May 1991 the Communist Party of Peru (Shining Path) (PCP) was reportedly responsible for killing Peruvian peasant leader Porfirio Suni Quispe, a bilingual educator, who had recently been elected a regional deputy. Amnesty International had adopted Porfirio Suni Quispe as a prisoner of conscience in May 1988, when he was detained for alleged involvement in terrorist activities. In fact, he appeared to have been arrested because of his support for local peasants involved in a land dispute with a state-owned enterprise. He was reportedly tortured to force him to sign a false confession.

When he was murdered, Porfirio Suni Quispe had been actively involved in the redis-

Peruvian peasant leader Porfirio Suni, shown here addressing members of the peasant community of Crucero, was adopted as a prisoner of conscience by Amnesty International in 1988. He was released, but in 1991 he was reportedly murdered by the PCP armed opposition group.

15

tribution of land to peasants in Puno. The groups he was assisting had resisted efforts by the PCP to take over their peasant movement and to recruit new members and carry out acts of violence in the region. At the funeral, the Bishop of Puno paid tribute to Porfirio Suni Quispe's dedication to indigenous people.

The death penalty

Amnesty International opposes the death penalty in all cases as a violation of the right to life and the right not to be subjected to cruel, inhuman or degrading punishment, as proclaimed in the Universal Declaration of Human Rights.

Amnesty International's campaign for the abolition of the death penalty in the USA began many years ago. It has involved worldwide appeals for the abolition of the death penalty, repeated representions to US officials, submissions to the UN and other international bodies, and the publication of numerous reports. In 1980, for example, Amnesty International published a proposal for a US Presidential Commission on the death penalty, in which it asked that the issue be examined from the perspectives of: international human rights and US constitutional rights and guarantees; racial discrimination in the imposition of the death penalty; the arbitrariness of indictments and prosecutions; the possibility of error; adequacy of legal representation of the poor; fairness of state clemency procedures; fairness of jury selection in death penalty cases; and the social consequences of the death penalty, including the impact of the death penalty on crime.

Some 45 Native Americans are now on death row in the USA out of a total US death row population of over 2,500. In most of these cases, the defendants were represented at trial by court-appointed lawyers; almost invariably, later investigation of cases by lawyers representing defendants in post-conviction appeals revealed extensive mitigating evidence, such as medical histories and details of family backgrounds which should have been presented during the trial.

As a matter of policy, Amnesty International calls for clemency whenever it fears that an execution is imminent. In January 1992 Amnesty International appealed for clemency for Anson Avery Maynard, a Coharie Indian who had been scheduled for execution in North Carolina on 17 January 1992 for the murder of a white man in 1981. Anson Avery Maynard had consistently maintained his innocence and, before his trial, had refused to plead guilty to second degree murder, even though it would have made him eligible for parole after 10 years. He was the sole person prosecuted for the murder. Another white man was granted immunity from prosecution, despite his admitted involvement in the crime. Amnesty International wrote to North Carolina Governor James Martin expressing its deep concern that Anson Avery Maynard's execution had been scheduled despite remaining doubts about the credibility of witness testimony used to convict him, and before his lawyers had an opportunity to seek a final review of his case in the US Supreme Court. Shortly before the scheduled execution, Governor Martin commuted the death sentence to life imprisonment without possibility of parole, on the grounds that there was "reasonable doubt as to whether the degree of involvement of Anson Maynard in the murder had been sufficiently clear to justify the death penalty". Five other Native Americans are on death row in North Carolina.

Several US studies have suggested that the death penalty is imposed in a discriminatory way, with homicides involving white victims more likely to result in death sentences than those whose victims are members of ethnic minority groups. In 1987 Amnesty International published *United States of*

Anson Avery Maynard, a Coharie Indian, was scheduled for execution in the USA in January 1992 for the murder of a white man. After worldwide appeals, his sentence was commuted to life imprisonment. ©Fayetteville Observer

America: The Death Penalty, a comprehensive report which showed that there were disparities based on racial factors in death sentencing throughout the USA. It has further been shown that the poor in the USA often do not have adequate legal representation generally and with respect to capital murder cases; American Indians are among the disadvantaged US minority groups.

The Death Penalty and Juvenile Offenders, an Amnesty International report published in October 1991, discussed the application of the death penalty in the USA to children or adolescents under the age of 18 at the time of their offence, in clear contravention of international human rights standards. The report described the cases of 23 juvenile offenders sentenced to death in the USA in recent years and also examined national history, law and practice regarding the execution of juveniles. Although no indigenous juvenile offenders were under sentence of death at the time of writing, historically race has been found to be a factor in the imposition of the death penalty on juveniles. According to data published in 1987, 75 per cent of all juvenile offenders executed since 1600 whose race was known belonged to non-white groups; three per cent were American Indians. The youngest children known to have been executed in US history were three 12-year-olds (two black slave boys and an American Indian girl) who were hanged in the late 18th century in the states of Connecticut, Virginia and Alabama. The youngest at the time of the crime was James Arcene, a 10-year-old Cherokee Indian who was convicted of killing a white man but evaded arrest for years and was hanged by the federal government in 1885.

Amnesty International is also concerned that those under sentence of death in the USA include many prisoners who are mentally impaired. An Amnesty International delegate visiting the USA in February 1992 found that Native Americans under sentence of death came overwhelmingly from acutely deprived social backgrounds. While convicted of very serious crimes, in many cases, there was evidence that they had been physically abused, neglected or abandoned as children. Many were found to suffer from mental illness or brain damage or very low IQ. Foetal alcohol syndrome was of concern in several cases. In two cases, murders appeared to have been linked to serious mental illnesses suffered by Native Americans who had served in the Viet Nam war. Alcohol dependency, drug abuse and addiction to inhalants and other chemical substances were found to be factors present in the commission of many of the crimes by lawyers who re-investigated the cases during the appeal process. However, such evidence was generally not introduced by the court-appointed lawyers who had represented the Native Americans at their original trials.

Amnesty International has frequently lobbied against federal death penalty bills in the USA which proposed the reintroduction of the death penalty for crimes, including homicide, committed on federal lands even in states that do not otherwise have the death penalty. Such legislation would discriminate against US Indians and Alaskan native people living on federal reservation lands, by subjecting them to the death penalty for crimes which did not carry a capital sentence elsewhere in the state. According to the US Sentencing Commission's 1988 *Annual Report*, over 75 per cent of all those sentenced for homicide in the federal courts between 1 November 1987 and 28 February 1989 were American Indians and Native Alaskans. In 1991 the US Senate approved a bill which would have expanded the death penalty to more than 50 federal crimes, but also agreed to let Indian tribal governments decide whether the death penalty should apply to offences committed by Indians within their jurisdiction. At the time of writing, this bill had not completed its passage through Congress, apparently on grounds other than the impact it would have on indigenous peoples.

Amnesty International also opposes the return or extradition of any person to a country where he or she could face the death penalty. In January 1992 the organization wrote to the Canadian Minister of Justice regarding the proposed extradition of a Canadian Abenaki Indian, Lee Robert O'Bomsawin, to Florida, USA, where he faced a charge of murder.

Between 1976, when US states revised their death penalty laws, and April 1992 Florida executed 27 prisoners: the second highest number executed in any state. In April 1992, 315 prisoners were under sentence of death in Florida, one of whom was believed to be a Native American. Further, studies have shown that racial discrimination is a factor in the imposition of the death penalty in the state. In its letter to the Canadian Minister of Justice, Amnesty International asked that, as a pre-condition of the extradition, assurances be sought from the Florida state authorities that the death penalty would not be imposed. In February 1992 it was announced that Lee Robert O'Bomsawin was to be extradited but that, at the insistence of the Canadian Government, the authorities in Florida had undertaken not to seek the death penalty.

'Disappearance'

Indigenous peoples have been among the tens of thousands of people who have "disappeared" in the Americas in recent decades. The use of "disappearance" to eliminate opponents and control dissent became widespread after the military coup in Chile in 1973 and in Argentina after 1976. Over the years, the practice has been reported from many other countries in the region. Today it continues in many parts of the Americas and remains widespread in Guatemala, Peru and Colombia, although these countries have returned to civilian governments.

Although it occurs elsewhere, over the last three decades the phenomenon of "disappearance" has often been associated with Latin America. The term was first used in its Spanish form of *desaparecido*, to describe a government policy of abducting real or perceived opponents on a massive scale in Guatemala since the 1960s.

"Disappearances" still occur in Guatemala. Those who "disappear" often seem to have been singled out because of their leadership role in indigenous or other movements. Luis Miguel Solís Pajarito, a leader of the National Council of Displaced People of Guatemala (CONDEG) has been missing since 3 May 1990. He was CONDEG's representative in the National Dialogue, a regional consultation process initiated by the presidents of Central America in August 1989. The National Dialogue was intended to negotiate the basis for a peaceful settlement to the armed conflicts then raging in the region. CONDEG works on behalf of the thousands of people displaced from their homes by army counter-insurgency sweeps. Luis Miguel Solís Pajarito was himself displaced, having fled to Guatemala City from his home in El Quiché after his father and three brothers "disappeared". He had received a series of threats and, several days before he went missing, he had narrowly escaped abduction by a group of men in civilian clothes. His wife, Rosa Pu, has worked both through the Mutual Support Group (GAM) and CONAVIGUA, the largely indigenous association of Guatemalan widows, to try to locate him. As a result, she has been followed and accosted by unknown men. In January 1992 she was threatened at gunpoint by a man in plain clothes. Other members of her family have also "disappeared". Her first husband was seized in 1981 and never seen again.

Evidence of the fate of some of the "disappeared" has emerged: violent, often illegal arrest; torture; secret imprisonment; death.

CONAVIGUA **member Rosa Pu, a Quiché Indian, has lost two husbands and a number of other relatives to "disappearance" in Guatemala.**

Testimonies of survivors, witnesses and sometimes of perpetrators has emerged in some countries not only to lay individual "disappearances" at the door of specific security agencies and agents, but also to prove that "disappearance" was an official policy intended to eliminate government opponents and terrorize the population, while evading accountability. Even when official responsibility for "disappearances" has been established, those responsible are rarely brought to justice.

The civilian government elected in Argentina in 1983 established a commission to clarify the fate of the thousands who "disappeared" during the previous seven years of military rule. The investigatory commission concluded that human rights had been systematically violated by the armed forces using state machinery and documented 8,960 cases of "disappearance". They included Chilean Mapuche Luis Quinchavil Suárez, detained in Argentina in February 1981 with another exiled Chilean, José Alejandro Campos Cifuentes, as the two were attempting to return clandestinely to Chile. They were never seen again. Both men had served prison terms in Chile under the military government of General Augusto Pinochet which overthrew the government of Salvador Allende in 1973. Luis Quinchavil Suárez had been arrested in Chile shortly after the military coup, reportedly because of his activities as a trade union and political activist in a left-wing political party specifically targeted by the new military government. His political activities had included involvement in repossessing Mapuche lands, a legal activity under the Allende government's agrarian reform program. Released on the condition that he go into exile, Luis Quinchavil Suárez worked as a teacher of the Mapuche language at Leiden University in the Netherlands, until his ill-fated attempt to return to Chile with José Campos Cifuentes.

After civilian government returned to Chile in 1990, the National Commission of Truth and Reconciliation (CNVR) was appointed to look into serious human rights violations committed during the years of military government. The CNVR examined the case of Luis Quinchavil and José Campos, and concluded that they had been arrested by Argentine police and handed over to the Chilean security forces, who were responsible for their "disappearance".

"Disappearance" has a devastating effect on the victims' families, who face prolonged and anguished uncertainty as to the fate of their relatives, yet cannot mourn their loss. Often widows cannot receive compensation or welfare support or may not be able

"Remember us after we have gone. Don't forget us. Conjure up our faces and our words. Our image will be as dew in the hearts of those who want to remember us". From the Popol Vuh, *sacred book of the Quiché Maya.
The walls of the Guatemala City office of GAM, the mutual support group for those whose relatives have "disappeared", are lined with photographs of the missing.*

to obtain passports, leave the country or remarry. Fifteen people from the small community of Liquiñe, Chile, many of them Mapuche Indians, "disappeared" after being seized by soldiers and police officers in 1973. Relatives only gained the courage to make a formal complaint about the "disappearances" 17 years later, after the return of civilian government. The wife of one of those who had "disappeared" told local human rights workers how the loss of her husband had affected her: "All these years I have had to live with hunger, poverty, exploitation, and above all fear, confusion, doubt, distrust, loss and loneliness".

Torture and ill-treatment

During the early days of colonization, according to historians, Indians could have their hands cut off if they failed to fill their gold quota or even touched a piece of Spanish clothing. In the Caribbean, Arawak Indians were suspended over fires of green wood, chosen intentionally as it burned more slowly and therefore prolonged the victims' agony. Contemporary accounts relate that one captain complained that he couldn't sleep because of the cries of those being slowly tortured to death; he ordered them strangled instead. At that time, Indian children were often thrown into the sea by soldiers who said they were "children of the devil"; chiefs and Indian nobles were burned to death on grids of iron.

Indigenous people in the Americas are tortured for a variety of reasons, ranging from attempts to extract money from them to forcing them to make false "confessions". Some have been tortured and ill-treated as a result of living in areas of conflict.

In Guyana, a 53-year-old Amerindian was brutally tortured with no apparent purpose other than to extract money from him. Anthony La Cruz was first taken into custody in 1986 after he had reported the theft of a saw he had borrowed from his neighbour. He was detained for three days and released on bail on payment of 600 Guyanese dollars, for which he was given no receipt. Two months later he was rearrested and according to his statement, brutally tortured for two days before being released on bail, this time of 400 Guyanese dollars. He said he was stripped and his feet placed in irons, beaten, and dragged about by a wire attached to his genitals and threatened he would be shot with a gun which was placed to his head. He said his jailors laughed as they warned him that his pubic hair would be burned off or pulled out, placed red hot pepper on his genitals, and forced him at gun-point to eat excrement from a lavatory bowl. He also testified that they subjected him to racial insults. After his release, it was reported that Anthony La Cruz displayed marks on his back, face and buttocks consistent with the treatment he had described. Unassimilated Amerindians in Guyana are estimated to number some 45,000. Guyanese parliamentarians have pointed to a number of cases of alleged ill-treatment of Amerindian detainees in recent years and have publicly suggested they may be particularly vulnerable to ill-treatment in custody.

Torture and ill-treatment in custody is widespread in Brazil, and many of the victims have died as a result. Velario Tamir Macuxí, a 17-year-old Macuxí Indian from northeast Roraima, was found dead in his cell in the Normandia police station in October 1988. He and two other Macuxí Indians had been arrested the night before by civil police officers after scuffles had broken out at an election rally. Other youths in custody at the same time said that they were all beaten and that Velario Tamir Macuxí appeared to have been particularly badly beaten. He reportedly called out for medical help, but the doctor on duty at the Normandia hospital was apparently not summoned, nor was he called to do an autopsy when Velario Tamir was found dead. In 1990 the Normandia military police commander told an Amnesty International delegate that four civil police officers had been charged with "bodily harm, followed by death" in connection with Velario Tamir's death, but could not say whether they had been suspended from active service pending the trial. By February 1991 the police charged had reportedly not appeared at any of the three court hearings set, and the case had effectively stalled.

An Amnesty International delegation visited Quebec province, Canada, in November 1990 to investigate allegations that several Mohawk Indians had been ill-treated in custody. They had been arrested by the Quebec police in August and September 1990 on criminal charges including possession of unlawful weapons and participation in a riot. The arrests occurred during a heated 11-week confrontation between armed Mohawks and the Canadian security forces during which a police officer was killed. The confrontation stemmed from a land dispute.

Mohawk Indian Ronald Cross, photographed in the custody of the Quebec police after his arrest by the Canadian army in September 1990. The top photograph was allegedly taken at 4:30am on 27 September, the photograph below over 12 hours later, at 5pm. Ronald Cross asserts that these photographs confirm his allegations that he was kicked and hit in police custody. He was detained during an armed confrontation over land between Canadian security forces and Mohawk Indians. In January 1992 he was found guilty of a number of charges arising from the confrontation and was sentenced to 52 months' imprisonment.

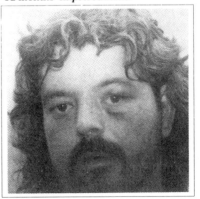

The Mohawks were protesting against proposals to build a golf course on land surrounding a Mohawk sacred burial site and had erected a roadblock between the towns of Oka and Châteauguay, near Montreal.

In 1991 Amnesty International wrote to the Quebec Minister of Justice, calling for investigation into six cases of alleged ill-treatment. One of the six detainees, Angus Jacobs, alleged that after his arrest in August 1990 he had been beaten and ill-treated by plainclothes members of the Quebec Security Police Force (SQ) and by officers from the Montreal Urban Community force. Another detainee, Ronald Cross, alleged that he had been kicked and hit by SQ officers in September 1990, after he had surrendered to the Canadian army. Medical reports and photographs were consistent with his allegations. Ronald Cross had been in the forefront of the Mohawk action. In January 1992 he was found guilty of a number of charges arising from the confrontation, including an attack on another Indian, and was later sentenced to 52 months' imprisonment. Amnesty International understands that his allegations of ill-treatment are now being investigated by the Quebec police ethics commissioner. Angus Jacobs' complaint is being studied by the Complaints Investigation Committee of the SQ. According to the Quebec Ministry of Justice in May 1992, the circumstances in which the police officer was killed remain under investigation.

In February 1992 Amnesty International wrote to the Director of the Department of Corrections in the state of Montana, USA, to place on record its concerns regarding the treatment of inmates of Montana State Penitentiary's (MSP) Maximum Security Unit, including Native Americans. According to the report of a US Justice Department inquiry team, when prison staff regained control after a riot in the unit in September 1991, prisoners were stripped, handcuffed, and forced to run a gauntlet of officers who punched, kicked and tripped them and hit them with batons. Amnesty International welcomed the decision of the Montana Corrections Department to commission an outside inquiry into the affair, and asked what steps had been taken to implement the investigators' recommendations regarding the policy on use of force, grievance and disciplinary systems and measures for reviewing and alleviating conditions in the Maximum Security Unit. The organization recognized the serious nature of the riot, and the extremely violent acts perpetrated by some inmates, which included the murder of five protective custody prisoners. However, it emphasized that the authorities are responsible for ensuring that prison personnel are fully aware of the requirement that inmates be treated humanely at all times.

Native Americans make up between 18 and 20 per cent of the inmates at MSP; they constitute only four per cent of Montana's population. Native American prisoners in MSP have complained of being verbally abused by the prison's predominantly white guards and treated more harshly than other inmates. They are also said to have been denied visits from their religious representatives and have not been allowed certain religious items. One Native American prisoner commented in January 1992 that "[the] administration here at the prison believe[s] that if we practised [our religion] it would be a security risk. Many white people here have a chaplain or a priest come to see them weekly; they have unlimited religious reading, rosary beads for confession and bible studies to help them grow spiritually.... The sacred pipe I have been denied access to as well as tobacco for prayers. I have not had an opportunity to speak to a medicine man or anyone for spiritual guidance". Amnesty International is not in a position to confirm these allegations. However, in its letter the organization asked the Director of Montana's Corrections Department for comments on these claims. A number of Native American prisoners in the USA have been forced to have their hair cut, contrary to their belief that this damages their spiritual well-being. Since 1987 a few US courts have ruled that special religious exemptions are a prisoner's right unless the prison has actual proof that they pose a security risk.

In situations of civil conflict, torture may be used by government agents to extract information from captives they believe to be engaged in "subversive" activities, or to have aided the armed opposition willingly or unwillingly, or simply because they did not report the presence of strangers in the area. People may also be tortured to dissuade others from joining, supporting or offering any logistical help to the armed opposition.

Torture is often a prelude to "disappearance" or extrajudicial execution and tortured bodies have been displayed in public to sow further terror. In 1980, 39 people, most of them indigenous, who had peacefully occupied the Spanish Embassy in Guatemala City to draw attention to army abuses in their home department of El Quiché, died when police and military personnel stormed the embassy. The sole indigenous survivor, Gregorio Yujá, was rescued with minor burns. However, he was later abducted from the hospital where he had been taken for treatment, and his tortured body thrown onto the campus university with a note interpreted as a warning to students and faculty there who had supported the Indians' protest.

During the counter-insurgency offensive in Guatemala in the late 1970s, tortured village activists were displayed to their fellow villagers as examples of what would happen to anyone whom the army believed had joined the armed opposition. One victim was 16-year-old community organizer Petrocino Menchú Tum. In September 1979 Petrocino Menchú was abducted and tortured for 16 days while in the custody of the Guatemalan military. Reportedly, stones were forced into his eyes, his finger-nails were pulled out, flesh was peeled from his face, the soles of his feet were sliced off, his tongue was amputated, and he was held in a well filled with corpses. The military then summoned the inhabitants from surrounding villages to come and see how "guerrillas" were punished; the villagers were told that they would suffer the same fate if they refused to come, or if they had anything to do with the armed opposition. They were then forced to watch as victims, including Petrocino Menchú, were further tortured and, finally, doused with petrol and set alight. Petrocino Menchú's sister, Rigoberta Menchú, is now an internationally renowned indigenous leader.

In situations of internal conflict, the armed opposition may also carry out acts of torture. In Peru, the PCP has sometimes tortured and mutilated its victims, including indigenous people, as a prelude to execution-style killings.

A wide variety of torture methods have been reported, ranging from savage beatings to electric shocks and mock executions. The rape of women is frequently reported, particularly in areas where the security forces are engaged in counter-insurgency operations. Some of the cruellest forms of torture are psychological; family members may be forced to stand by as their loved ones are tortured, or are threatened that their relatives will be killed.

In a testimony given to Amnesty International after he escaped from the Guatemalan military base where he had been detained and tortured after his abduction in 1981, indigenous leader Emeterio Toj Medrano said that in addition to the physical torture to which he was subjected — including confinement in an oven, electric shock treatment, continual hooding and prolonged sleep and food deprivation — one of the hardest things to bear had been the threats directed at his family. "The army gave me not only physical blows but also psychological blows ... They tried to demoralize me ... They threatened to murder my family in Huehuetenango. They told me that they had already kidnapped them, that they had all the children and my wife and they would undress her and the girls in order to rape them in front of me, and that they were going to start killing them one by one, starting with the youngest girls.... They also threatened to massacre, and in fact they did massacre the villages and towns where I was working. They also threatened to do away with the indigenous peoples in the west." Emeterio Toj Medrano also said that he had repeatedly been injected with drugs, apparently to induce him to cooperate with his captors who wished him to denounce indigenous and church organizations as linked to subversion.

Arbitrary detention and unfair trial

In several countries in the Americas, indigenous peoples have been arbitrarily detained or imprisoned after unfair trials, sometimes on false charges.

In December 1991 Ch'ol and Tzeltal indigenous communities in the state of Chiapas, Mexico, staged a peaceful demonstration protesting against police abuse of Indians and discrimination in the legal system. They charged that indigenous people were forced to pay bribes for services in the corrupt local civil courts. They also claimed they were not provided with lawyers or interpreters during court proceedings; in May 1991 the Mexican Government had assured the UN Committee on the Elimination of Racial Discrimination that lawyers and interpreters were always provided.

Over 100 of the Indians who demonstrated were reportedly kicked, beaten and threatened with death after being arrested. They remained *incommunicado* for over 30 hours, without food or medical care. Most were released on the following days, but they were warned to abandon their protest or face rearrest. The remaining nine detainees were imprisoned for several weeks under reportedly false charges. For example, Manuel Martínez Pérez, a 25-year-old Ch'ol Indian activist, was charged with murder, despite the fact that several witnesses, including relatives of his alleged victim, testified that he had nothing to do with the crime and had been arrested because of mistaken identity. He also had an apparently well-founded alibi placing him elsewhere at the time of the crime. He was released free of charges on 1 April 1992 following growing national and international pressure for his immediate and unconditional release.

In the USA, Russell Means, one of the leaders of the American Indian Movement (AIM), the activist Indian rights group, was a prisoner of conscience when he was imprisoned in 1977. He was arrested after participating in a meeting regarding relations between the white and Indian communities of Sisseton, South Dakota, on the grounds that this infringed a bail order stipulating that he could not participate in AIM political activities. This bail order had by its nature infringed Russell Means' fundamental rights to freedom of expression and association, rights which are also protected under the US Constitution. He was released later in 1977 by order of the Federal Court of Appeal, which declared the original bail order constitutionally invalid.

There have been instances in which prosecutions in non-capital cases in the USA appear to have been initiated for political reasons. Amnesty International documented misconduct by the Federal Bureau of Investigation (FBI) during a 1981 operation code-named COINTELPRO. This was an intelligence investigation into the activities of domestic political groups, and although it was officially denied at the time, it is widely alleged that AIM was one of the groups investigated. Amnesty International identified instances where AIM members and others appeared to have been falsely charged with criminal offences, selectively prosecuted or deprived of due legal process for reasons of race or political activities. It found that in several such cases the FBI had acted improperly and had thereby apparently attempted to prejudice the right to a fair trial of AIM members charged with serious offences.

In several countries, indigenous people have been arbitrarily imprisoned after unfair trials because of their suspected support for government opponents. After the fall of Anastasio Somoza, Nicaragua's long-term ruler, in 1979 the new *Sandinista* Government took steps to assert its control over the Atlantic Coast, a region increasingly infiltrated by the armed Nicaraguan resistance, known as the *Contra*, forces who were operating with the backing of the US Government. Several indigenous groups, whose members included Miskito, Sumo and Rama Indians in the region, joined forces with the Contra and took up arms against the *Sandinista* Government.

In late 1981 the *Sandinista* Government declared a state of emergency in northern Zelaya department in response to a *Contra* offensive. Some 200 people, most of them Miskito Indians, were detained near the border with Honduras. According to Miskito and church sources, the Indians were detained because the authorities believed they had supported *Contra* activities in the region. In some cases the alleged complicity consisted of having given food to the armed rebels. Some 135 of the detainees, largely Miskito and Sumo Indians, were later convicted of crimes under the Law for the Maintenance of Public Order and Security. This law, passed in 1979, defined crimes and prescribed sentences which were applied not just to violent opponents of the government, but to non-violent critics of its policies as well. Amnesty International was concerned at the detention, summary trial procedures and limited right to defence allowed Indians and others taken into custody by the *Sandinista* Government under the terms of the law.

Complaints were also made regarding the conduct of the trials; only three public defenders were assigned to the 135 defendants, and proceedings were conducted in Spanish, although some of those on trial spoke only Miskito. However, many of these prisoners were later released under amnesty laws passed by the *Sandinista* Government, some of which were intended to benefit indigenous people convicted of political crimes.

In a number of countries it has also been reported that indigenous people have been held for long periods without being charged or tried because neither they nor their families have the resources to obtain legal assistance or do not understand the reasons for their arrest and detention, or what is required to bring the case to trial or for the detainee to be released. This can make them vulnerable to conviction and more severe sentencing in criminal cases. In the late 1970s and early 1980s Amnesty International raised its concern with the Mexican authorities on several occasions about reports that many hundreds of indigenous people had been arbitrarily arrested and were being held without trial in jails in remote areas of Mexico, from which it was difficult to obtain details; prison conditions were reportedly severely substandard, and detainees routinely subjected to torture and ill-treatment.

Indigenous people often report that they are detained on criminal charges in order to mask attempts by the authorities working with private commercial interests to remove them from their lands or destroy their community organizations. In 1984 and 1985 Amnesty International found that Triqui Indians in Oaxaca, southern Mexico, had been imprisoned on criminal charges on the basis of dubious evidence, consisting mainly of uncorroborated testimony. Long delays in trial proceedings meant that many people were imprisoned for lengthy periods before their eventual release. It was believed that the real reason for the Indians' arrests were their efforts to protect Triqui lands.

State and commercial interests have also been accused of fomenting conflict between different indigenous groups, in order that those who oppose local landowners or state political programs can be detained on criminal charges and so removed from the scene.

Apparently unfounded charges of involvement in the 1990 murder of a local landowner were brought against 13 members of the Mixe and Zapotec community of La Trinidad Yaveo, Oaxaca. The landowner had apparently been killed by inhabitants of a neighbouring community who had confrontations with him on a number of occasions, stemming from a personal dispute. It is believed that the Indians from La Trinidad Yaveo were charged with the crime because of their involvement in a community group, the Organized Communal Work Group (TCO). The TCO was trying to retain the community's lands, and to keep alive its cultural traditions, language and communal work practices. However, local landowners who are said to have seized large tracts of land for cattle grazing and for cultivating cannabis have allegedly tried to destroy the TCO by encouraging other members of the indigenous community to form a rival group.

On 25 January 1992, a joint squad of police officers and local gunmen carried out another raid on the community of La Trinidad Yaveo. In the course of the raid, a Mixe Indian, Tomás Diego García, was summarily executed, two women were reportedly beaten with weapons and one state judicial police officer allegedly put the barrel of his gun into the mouth of five-year-old Misael García Santiago and threatened to kill him if he did not stop crying. Five Mixes and one Zapotec were arrested in connection with the 1990 murder of the landowner.

There were serious irregularities in proceedings against the six detainees. There were apparently illegal delays in bringing them before a judge and they were allegedly beaten and ill-treated by having hot candle wax poured over their hands. Reportedly, the judge refused to record their allegations that they had signed confessions under torture. One was later released; the remaining five were charged with murder. When Amnesty International visited the five detainees in prison in February 1992, one of its delegates, a medical doctor with forensic experience, found signs consistent with the torture they said they had suffered.

Eight other members of the community had been detained on the same charges in July 1990 and sentenced in December 1991 to 25 years' imprisonment on the basis of what they claim are unfounded accusations and confessions made under torture. Amnesty International believed that the 13 detained members of the Mixe-Zapotec community at La Trinidad Yaveo were prisoners of conscience, arbitrarily detained because of their peaceful activities on behalf of their community. After worldwide appeals, all of the Indians from La Trinidad Yaveo were released in 1992.

2

No one is safe: the targets of abuses

Indigenous peoples in all parts of the Americas have suffered human rights abuses. Victims include community and religious leaders, children and the elderly. Others have suffered abuses because of their work to strengthen indigenous culture or revive pride in their traditional ways. No sector of indigenous society has been spared.

Human rights abuses against indigenous people often arise out of disputes over land and resource use or ownership.

Indigenous peoples caught up in civil conflict have suffered brutal violations on a mass scale. Whole communities have been massacred on suspicion that they sympathised with the armed opposition.

The "war against drugs" has claimed many indigenous people among its victims. Many live in areas where there is conflict between drug traders, often backed by corrupt military and police commanders, armed opposition groups seeking to use illegal crops to finance their activities and police forces said to be trying to destroy the coca harvest.

Indigenous peoples are often more vulnerable to abuses and less able to seek redress than others in their societies because of racial prejudice and discrimination. Discrimination may also be reflected in the criminal justice system.

The struggle for land and resources

"As long as water flows, or grass grows upon the earth, or the sun rises to show your pathway, or you kindle your camp fires, so long shall you be protected by this government and never again be removed from your present habitations."

Senator Sam Houston of Texas, USA, in a discourse to the US Congress in 1854, describing what was to have been the perpetual nature of the reservations created for US Indians.

Disputes over the ownership of land and resources have frequently given rise to human rights violations against indigenous people. Disputes can occur when state or commercial interests seek to exploit traditional indigenous lands for mining, logging, hydro-electric or tourism projects. In some cases human rights violations have followed state and private development of land officially designated as indigenous, in defiance of laws protecting those lands. In several countries, long-running land disputes, where the legal basis of land ownership is not clear, or where earlier land agreements between central government and indigenous popula-tions have been overturned, have left a legacy of human rights violations. Amnesty International does not take sides in disputes over land and resource use or ownership, but is concerned about specific human rights violations that occur in such contexts.

Brazil's new Constitution of 1988 guarantees Indians' inalien-able rights to their traditional lands, proclaiming that: "The social

Tzotzil Indians of Mexico — the slogan reads "This land has been paid for with our blood".

35

organization, customs, languages, beliefs and traditions of Indians are recognized, as are their original rights to the lands they traditionally occupy. The nation must demarcate and protect these lands and ensure the respect of Indian property. This has encouraged indigenous groups to actively claim land they believe to be theirs. It is often precisely when Indian groups attempt to exercise the right to the lands they claim that they suffer abuses. The Brazilian authorities have consistently failed to prevent the abuses or to investigate them effectively. The 1988 Constitution provides for demarcation of all Indian lands by 1993, but this goal seems unlikely to be achieved. Significant delays in promised demarcation have been noted in Brazil in the past; its Indian Statute of 1973 had provided for the demarcation of all Indian lands by 1978. The ILO, commenting on the government's degree of compliance with Convention 107 on Indigenous and Tribal Populations to which Brazil is a party, observed in 1988 that the slowness of the demarcation process "at times provokes radical situations which sometimes result in conflicts".

Damião Mendes' body was found by his sister on 25 June 1990. The 35-year-old Macuxí Indian was lying face down in the mud of a river bank. He had been shot in the back of the neck. Nearby lay the body of his nephew, 19-year-old Mario Davis. Both men came from the Macuxí settlement of Santa Cruz near Normandia, a town on the border between Roraima, Brazil's most northern state, and French Guiana.

The Macuxí are a semi-nomadic group of an estimated 15,000 Indians, living on the plains of Roraima, whose claim to these ancestral lands is contested by cattle ranchers. The killing of Damião Mendes and Mario Davis fell into a pattern of repeated attacks on the Macuxí Indians of Santa Cruz, which intensified after the Indians began to press their claim to land they believed to be theirs. The Macuxí community lies on land claimed by the largest private estate in the area, the Fazenda Guanabara.

The basic facts of this case are far from exceptional: dozens of Indians in Brazil have been murdered in similar circumstances. Damião Mendes and Mario Davis were killed because of a land dispute. The investigation into the killing was cursory. No one has been brought to justice.

The estate manager is the man believed to be responsible for the killings. He allegedly told two other Indians: "I killed two Indians, they're dead and I'm not sorry. I shall give myself up to the police like a man".The day after the killings the farm manager presented himself at the police station. His statement was taken and he was immediately released. Police only visited the scene of the crime two days later, after the bodies had been brought to the village and inspected by a police doctor in preparation for burial. The farm manager reportedly returned to the Indian area a few days later and threatened the dead men's relatives: "I've already killed two, and I shall kill more". After protests from the independent Indigenous Council of Roraima, CIR, federal police took over the case and the manager was taken into custody in Bõa Vista. He subsequently alleged that he was tortured by police after he had confessed to the crime. In March 1991 the farm manager was released from custody: he returned to the Fazenda Guanabara.

In Venezuela, there have been a number of accounts regarding abuses directed against members of indigenous groups in the context of disputes over land. For example, in 1982 members of the Piaroa Indian community of Caño Vera Guanay in Amazonas, Venezuela, were reportedly the victims of arrests, ill-treatment and intimidation by police and private ranch guards. A funeral procession had tried to cross land claimed by a private company on their way to a traditional burial ground. Part of the land claimed by the ranchers had been adjudicated to the Piaroa community by the state. Private guards allegedly seized two members of the Piaroa funeral party and beat and whipped them. Agents of the civilian police (DISIP) reportedly arrived on the scene in response to radio reports from ranch employees that they were in danger of being attacked by the Piaroa Indians. Reportedly, the police then inflicted further beatings on the two captives. The two Indians were then taken to the provincial capital, Puerto Ayacucho. They were released after National Guard officers observed that they had been badly beaten and refused to accept responsibility for their detention. Charges were brought against five ranch employees for illegally detaining and wounding the Indians, but the judge hearing the case ordered their release on what the then Venezuelan Attorney General described as questionable grounds. Inquiries were also announced into the actions of the DISIP agents, but to Amnesty International's knowledge, they were not prosecuted.

On 24 December 1991 Florencio Cáceres, a leader of the San Esteban tribe in Yoro Province, Honduras, was shot dead, allegedly by a local landowner who claimed title to land the San Esteban were working. He was the ninth leader of the indigenous organization the Federation of Xicaque Tribes of Yoro (FETRIXY) to have been killed in four years. The president of FETRIXY, Vicente Matute Cruz, was shot dead in September 1991. A prominent indigenous leader, he had publicly declared that civilians, members of the military and government personnel had unlawfully seized land belonging to indigenous communities. FETRIXY was formed to defend indigenous rights, such as the right to Xicaque lands which it charges have been illegally occupied. FETRIXY believes that all nine killings were ordered by landowners involved in land disputes with FETRIXY members. No one has been brought to justice for any of these killings, nor does it appear that they have been properly investigated. This raises concern that those responsible for the killings may be operating with the complicity or acquiescence of local authorities.

Human rights violations have occurred when traditional lands or resources are sought for government defence or energy projects, in which case a "national security interest" may be asserted for depriving Indians of their land, encouraging others to drive them from it, and condoning abuses against them. Sometimes the fact the Indians live in areas that now cross national

Vicente Matute Cruz, President of the Federation of the Xicaque Tribes of Yoro, was shot dead in September 1991 by armed men believed to be acting for local landowners. He had publicly declared that civilians, members of the military and government personnel had unlawfully seized land belonging to indigenous communities.

Waxi Saluma, one of the survivors of the attack on Holomai village, near Brazil's border with Venezuela, was still suffering from gunshot injuries when interviewed by Amnesty International one year later.

When did the war begin?
Who knows when the war
began.
Do you know when the war
began?
When the war began
We did not know why they
killed us
Or how long they killed us
Or how long they had been
killing us
But how they killed us!
from The Hour of our People,
by Jacinto Galileo

borders has led governments to tolerate or encourage settlement by non-indigenous peoples to secure national frontiers. Colonization of these areas sometimes conflicts with laws and treaties giving indigenous peoples the right to the lands. Settlers have often committed abuses against indigenous people which the state has been unable or unwilling to control.

Amnesty International has received a number of reports of Yanomami Indians, in Brazil, being killed by gold miners and settlers. In one case the Indians were attacked after being drawn into a dispute between rival groups of gold miners. In September 1990 Lourenço Yekuana, a 65-year-old village léader and his son were shot and killed by armed miners who attacked their village, Holomai, in the Auaris region near the Venezuelan border. The attack followed a conflict between rival groups of miners who were contesting control of a mine in Auaris. One group had incited the Indians to charge the others for use of an airstrip illegally built on Yanomami territory. When the miners refused to pay, the Yanomami stole their goods. The attack on the Holomai village followed in reprisal.

A federal police investigation was opened but, reflecting the pattern of virtual impunity enjoyed by those who carry out attacks on Indians in Brazil, none of the 10 men accused were arrested. Their leader was briefly detained in May 1991 in Bõa Vista, capital of Roraima State, after he drew a gun on a group of Maingong Indians and shouted at them: "You Indians are like dogs, to be killed".

'Between the sword and the wall'

Victims of civil conflict

In a number of countries, indigenous communities living in areas of armed conflict have been targeted by both government forces and insurgent groups because they were believed to be sympathetic to one side or the other, or simply because they were resident in areas of conflict. Thousands of indigenous people have been killed or "disappeared" simply because they lived in areas of conflict. These communities have suffered selective killings, collective reprisals and unprovoked massacres carried out by both parties to the conflict.

Amnesty International called for inquiries into abuses against indigenous people in the context of the armed conflict in Nicaragua. One of the incidents which the organization believes has never been adequately clarified occurred in December 1981, following a series of cross-border raids carried out by the *Contra* opposition forces, their first significant military activity in the Atlantic Coast region of the country. When government forces regained control of the area, they reportedly found that seven captured *Sandinista* soldiers had been tortured and killed. Government forces then took a number of local people (estimates vary from 12 to as high as 80) into custody at Leimus, a Coco River settlement, as suspected collaborators with the *Contra*. Some of the prisoners, largely Miskito Indians, were summarily executed; others apparently died while trying to escape across the Coco River. Testimony given in the course of an investigation conducted by the *Sandinista* Ministry of the Interior, which included an account from a soldier present during the incident, indicated that 22 prisoners were summarily executed; other sources suggest that the figure may have been much higher. To Amnesty International's knowledge, those responsible have not been brought to justice.

During the 1980s Amnesty International also received frequent reports that the *Contra* forces, including several groups of Miskito, Sumo and Rama Indians, were responsible for torture and execution-style killing. Among the indigenous victims of these abuses were Miskito Indians José Cornejo and his wife, reportedly captured and killed by the *Contra* in late January 1984 near the hamlet of Yulo, on the grounds that they had cooperated with the Nicaraguan authorities.

In Colombia, Luis Napoleón Torres, an Arhuaco *mamo*, religious leader, and a governor of the Arhuaco Indians for seven years, was abducted, tortured and murdered in November 1990, along with his brother Angel María Torres, and another Arhuaco leader. The Arhuaco Indians are one of three indigenous groups living in the Sierra Nevada de Santa Marta mountains in northeast Colombia. At the time of their abduction, the three Arhuacos had been travelling to the capital, Bogotá, to denounce abuses being carried out against their communities by the army and police. At the time of writing, 18 months after the killings, two army officers implicated in their deaths remain in active service. The local police captain who failed to investigate when their "disappearance" was first reported to him has reportedly been promoted. The abuses reportedly stemmed from the army's suspicion that the Arhuaco community had been involved in the unsolved kidnapping six months earlier of a wealthy local landowner and farmer, apparently carried out by guerrilla forces. Although the Arhuaco community has rejected the guerrilla presence on its territory, and called unsuccessfully for official protection from them, the armed opposition has sometimes reportedly hidden its kidnap victims in Arhuaco reserves.

The Quechua and Aymara-speaking peasants who live in small agricultural communities in Peru's Andean highlands have also suffered abuses from both sides in the internal armed conflict which has racked the country for over a decade. Indigenous peoples, including children, have been among the thousands of victims. Some of the killings have been selective: their victims were community or trade union leaders and human rights activists. Other killings appear to be carried out as a means of collective punishment or intimidation of communities believed to be sympathetic to or supporting armed opposition activities in their area.

These abuses have continued since President Alberto Fujimori took office in July 1990. Between then and the end of April 1992, 392 people had reportedly "disappeared" and 169 had reportedly been extrajudicially executed. Many of these abuses occurred in the "emergency zones" under military control, where a large proportion of the population is indigenous.

The armed opposition in Peru, principally the clandestine PCP, has also killed thousands of people in Peru's coastal and rainforest regions. Many of the victims were indigenous people who opposed the PCP's political ideology and program. PCP captives are frequently tortured and subjected to mock trials before they are murdered.

A commission on which Peru's Ministers of Labour, Justice and Agriculture were represented, described the estimated 100,000 Indians living in the Peruvian Amazon as the living frontier. The region is considered to be of geo-political importance in Peru's internal conflict, and of economic importance because of its natural resources. The military, armed opposition groups — the PCP and the Túpac Amaru Revolutionary Movement (MRTA) — and drug traffickers have increased their activities in part of the region, and have allegedly been responsible for attacks on Ashaninka Indians.

The Ashaninkas are the largest of some 60 indigenous groups in the Peruvian Amazon. Several of their leaders have been killed; villages have been attacked and their inhabitants randomly and brutally murdered. On a number of occasions the opposition groups have allegedly acted with the cooperation of drug traffickers who are also reportedly moving into the area. In response, the government has forced the Indians to join army-backed self-defence militias, promising that this will help them reclaim their lands from PCP control. Those who refuse to join the militias have reportedly "disappeared" or been extrajudicially executed. The participation of some Ashaninka Indians in these patrols and the reported cooperation of others with the PCP has led to conflicts both within the group and between the Ashaninka and other indigenous groups in the area. It also appears to have marked the Ashaninka out for further PCP attacks. Caught between the opposing sides, numerous Ashaninka Indians have abandoned their homes and fled for their lives.

In response to queries from journalists about Amnesty International's reporting of atrocities by the Guatemalan army in 1982 an official spokesperson stated: "The guerrillas won over many Indian collaborators. There the Indians were subversives. And how do you fight subversives? Clearly you had to kill Indians because they were collaborating with subversives".

Successive governments in Guatemala have blamed atrocities on the armed opposition. On one occasion, foreign journalists investigating the massacre of 15 Indian peasants, three children of whom were children, in June 1982 in the village of Las Pacayas,

43

Alta Verapaz, a civil patroller translating survivors' statements into Spanish for foreign journalists said that the armed opposition had been responsible for the killings. However, the Indians' statement in Pokomchí had been recorded, and foreign ethnologists who listened to the tape later said that the Indians had actually blamed the army. According to some reports, government agents also bought indigenous clothing for troops to wear when carrying out attacks which could then be blamed on indigenous people said to have joined the armed opposition.

Victims of the 'drugs wars'

At least 20 Paez Indians were massacred near the town of Caloto, in the Cauca department of Colombia, on 16 December 1991. Some 60 hooded gunmen burst into a building where the Indians were holding a community meeting and opened fire on them. The dead included women and children. Indian communities in the northern Cauca area are attempting to recover traditional lands which they claim were assigned and titled to them when Colombia was a Spanish colony. Some communities have occupied land which they claim falls within their reservation. This has brought them into conflict with local landowners, some of

Funeral of the 20 Paez Indians massacred in Colombia by gunmen in December 1991

whom are allegedly involved in the drugs trade. Landowners in dispute with the Indians have waged a campaign of intimidation and harassment against them, with the assistance of paramilitary groups and the apparent support of the security forces.

The massacred Indians were members of the El Paez community, who had occupied a property known as "El Nilo", in the fertile Cauca river valley, since 1987. Their claims to the land have been contested by a succession of landowners. The killings followed a pattern of harassment and abuse against the Indians by gunmen apparently employed by landowners and drug traffickers said to have purchased the disputed land from its former owner two months earlier. The Paez community had repeatedly reported the harassment they were suffering to the authorities but no action was taken to investigate the threats, or to protect them.

Judicial investigations into the massacre were immediately opened; the Colombian Congress set up a special commission of inquiry and some civilians reported to be members of a paramilitary organization were arrested. However, the killings continued. One month after the massacre two lawyers who had been conducting an independent investigation of the incident were killed. Professor Edgar Torres and Rodolfo Alvarez were shot dead in their homes in Cali on 8 January 1992. Anthropologist Etnio Vidardo, who was also involved in the independent investigation, "disappeared" that night. In May 1992 another man who had been trying to help the Paez Indians was killed. Oscar Elias López, a lawyer working for the Regional Indigenous Council of the Cauca (CRIC), was shot dead by heavily armed gunmen in the town of Santander de Quilichao on 29 May. He had been acting as legal adviser to the Indians affected by the massacre and had reported receiving numerous death threats.

Judicial officials investigating the massacre have reportedly stated that suspects had claimed that members of the National Police, including the local police chief, were among those responsible. However, the results of the investigation have not been made public. Although there have been many investigations of suspected human rights violations in Colombia, only exceptionally do they lead to the prosecution of those responsible.

The remote areas in which some groups of indigenous people live are also sometimes used as smuggling routes by drug traffickers or for drug refinement. Some of the indigenous communities in these regions use unrefined coca leaves in religious ceremonies or as a normal part of their traditional way of life. Coca leaves are chewed not only to combat fatigue, hunger or thirst, and for medicinal reasons, but also have an important ritual role in traditional indigenous religious ceremonies. To the extent that coca is processed by local peasants, peasant unions say it is to make jams, biscuits, soft drinks and teas, rather than the intensively refined cocaine.

The fact that they live in coca producing regions, and that coca is a part of their daily lives, has rendered some indigenous peasant communities and coca producers' union leaders vulnerable to charges that they are involved in trafficking of cocaine or are offering safe havens to drugs smugglers or producers. Although this may be true in some cases, particularly when impoverished peasants may turn to coca production as a reliable cash crop, indigenous leaders allege that as attempts to eradicate coca production and cocaine trafficking intensify, with US assistance in parts of the region, such charges are often a pretext for officially sanctioned abuses against indigenous peoples.

In June 1989 Bolivian special patrol forces apprehended Evo Morales, a Quechua indigenous leader and secretary general of a peasant union in Cochabamba, central Bolivia. Interviewed by Amnesty International in 1991, Evo Morales said that he had been detained for allegedly protecting a drug trafficker, charges which he denied, and that he had been tortured by the Bolivian police. He said he was detained again in 1991, apparently because of his prominent role in a "march for dignity", organized by largely indigenous peasants to demand respect for their rights and demilitarization of their lands.

In October 1991 a Kuna Indian spokesperson told Amnesty International that Kuna communities had asked the Panamanian Government to take steps to protect them from drug traffickers moving into areas bordering Colombia, but that this had not been done. He said that indigenous people in Panama had already suffered indiscriminate attacks carried out by the traffickers and members of the Panamanian security forces working with them.

Victims of discrimination and deprivation

The plight of indigenous peoples in the Americas attracted widespread international attention in 1967 when 18 Cueva Indians from Colombia's Amazon jungle were killed by a small group of cattle ranchers who had moved illegally onto the Cueva home-lands. Later arrested and brought to trial, the ranchers admitted the killings, but questioned the charges. The Cueva were Indians, they argued, and everyone knew that Indians were animals, not people. There was even a verb in Colombian Spanish, *cuevar*, that meant "to hunt Cueva Indians". The jury found the ranchers innocent by reason of "cultural ignorance". But media attention on the trial put pressure on the Colombian Government to reopen the case; at their second trial, the ranchers were found guilty of murder and given lengthy prison sentences.

In 1987 the UN published the concluding chapters of a 22-volume study on the problem of discrimination against indigenous popu-lations. José Martínez Cobo of Cuba, the Special Rapporteur who carried out the study, declared: "the social conditions in which the majority of indigenous populations lived were favourable to the specific types of discrimination, oppression and exploitation in various fields described in the study. In many countries they are at the bottom of the socio-economic scale. They do not have the same opportunities for employment and the same access as other groups to public services and/or protection in the fields of health, living conditions, culture, religion and the administration of justice. They could not participate meaningfully in political life". Also in 1987, the Independent Commission on International Humanitarian Issues, a Geneva-based group which aims to stimulate governmen-tal and UN action on humanitarian problems, observed: "The present situation of indigenous peoples is rooted in their colo-nial past. If they are largely landless, underprivileged and dis-criminated against, it is because of the relationship of conqueror and conquered which was established during the early years of colonial contact".

It has been asserted that the prejudice, discrimination and social and economic deprivation which many indigenous peoples suffer in the Americas has led to discrimination in the criminal justice system, making them more likely to be unfairly tried, and to receive disproportionately severe sentences. At the same time, racial prejudice can result in a lack of official respect for Indian lives and Indian culture, and a consequent abuse of authority by state agents.

Amnesty International is able to act on cases affected by dis-crimination in the criminal justice system when they involve specific violations within the organization's mandate, including cruel, inhuman or degrading treatment, the detention of prisoners of conscience, unfair trials of political prisoners, or people sentenced to death.

One case in Canada where racial discrimination was found to have been a factor was that of Micmac Indian Donald Marshall Junior, convicted of murder in Nova Scotia in 1971. He was released in 1982 after new evidence emerged that another man had been responsible for the crime. A Royal Commission which examined the case found that there had been errors and misconduct by the prosecution, and that "seemingly unconscious racism and racial stereotyping" played a part in Donald Marshall's conviction, which had occurred, "in part at least, because he was a native person".

In Canada, government research in a number of provinces suggests that general prejudice against Native Canadians has led to discrimination in the justice system. An official study, the Aboriginal Justice Inquiry of Manitoba, noted that aboriginal people were less than 12 per cent of Manitoba's population, but at least 50 per cent of its prisoners. In 1991 the two senior judicial officials heading the Aboriginal Justice Inquiry reported: "The justice system has failed Manitoba's Aboriginal people on a massive scale. It has been insensitive and has arrested and imprisoned Aboriginal people in grossly disproportionate numbers". They also observed that "Aboriginal people who are arrested are more likely than non-Aboriginal people to be denied bail, spend more time in pretrial detention and spend less time with their lawyers, and, if convicted, are more likely to be incarcerated".

It has also been found that the rigour with which the Canadian police investigate crimes may depend on the race of the victim. Helen Betty Osborne, a 19-year-old Cree Indian from the Norway House community in Winnipeg, Manitoba province, was murdered in 1971. It was not until 1986, 16 years later, that one of the four men implicated in her killing was sentenced to life imprisonment for murder. Another was acquitted, one received immunity in return for testifying against the two tried for murder; the fourth was never charged. The Aboriginal Justice Inquiry reported in 1991 that several aspects of the police investigation were marred by racist attitudes; that Helen Betty Osborne's murder was motivated by racism; that neither the Department of Indian Affairs nor the Royal Canadian Mounted Police (RCMP) had exercised due vigilance to protect young Indian women from the racial and sexual harassment which they were known to suffer in The Pas, the town where the girl was murdered; and that the jury, which had no Aboriginal members, was not representative of the community where the trial was held.

The Aboriginal Justice Inquiry also examined the case of John Joseph Harper, a member of the Wasagamack Indian group and one of the leaders of Manitoba's Aboriginal community, who was killed in March 1988 in disputed circumstances. John Joseph Harper, who was unarmed, was killed during a struggle with a police officer when the officer's gun discharged. At the inquest into John Joseph Harper's death the judge found that the shooting was accidental and exonerated the police officer.

The Aboriginal Justice Inquiry, however, found that "racism played a part in the shooting of J.J. Harper and the events that followed ... [the police officer] was motivated to confront Harper primarily because of Harper's race". The inquiry concluded "that the City of Winnipeg Police Department did not search actively or aggressively for the truth about the death of J.J. Harper. Their investigation was, at best, inadequate. At worst, its primary objective seems to have been to exonerate [the police officer] and to vindicate the Winnipeg police department. We believe that evidence was mishandled and facts were obscured by police attempts to construct a version of events which would, in effect, blame J.J. Harper for his own death ... The Police Chief pre-empted the possibility of an effective investigation by exonerating [the police officer] prematurely and unjustifiably. His conduct was just the visible expression of an attitude which was prevalent in his department — an attitude which viewed the public image of the police department and the interests of one of its officers as more important than finding out the truth about the death of a citizen". The inquiry made a series of recommendations, including proper and more independent methods of investigating officer-involved shootings, and cross-cultural awareness training programs for police officers.

In the USA, Patrick Croy, a Shasta Native American, his sister, Norma Jean Croy, and three others were charged in 1978 with the murder of a white police officer in Yreka, Siskiyou County, California. Patrick and Norma Jean Croy were tried jointly in 1979. Patrick Croy was found guilty of first-degree murder and intentional killing of a police officer, and was sentenced to death. There was no evidence that Norma Jean Croy had fired a gun in the course of the incident. According to her testimony, she had been shot in the back as she tried to flee from the police. However, she was convicted of first-degree murder for aiding and abetting her brother, who fired the fatal shot, and sentenced to an indeterminate term of seven years to life imprisonment.

The California Supreme Court reversed Patrick Croy's conviction on the grounds that the jury had not been properly instructed. The Siskiyou County District Attorney's office then decided to try him again, and again to seek the death penalty. However, after hearing evidence that anti-Indian prejudice was endemic in the rural counties of Northern California, the judge granted a motion to change the trial venue, ruling that "The potential for residual bias against the defendant from preconceived notions about Native Americans ... raises a risk that prejudice will arise during the presentation of evidence".

The retrial was held in San Francisco, where the jury heard defence evidence that the police had used unreasonable or excessive force in pursuing the Croys and three other Native Americans after a minor incident at a liquor store, and that Patrick Croy honestly and reasonably believed his life was in danger when he fired the shot that killed the police officer.

Sociologists testified to the existence of racial tensions between the Native American and white communities in Yreka since the mid-1800s, when gold had been discovered and non-Indian settlers and miners moved into the area. The court heard that, during a 20-year-period between 1848 and 1868, some 120,000 Indians were murdered. The accounts of these killings are apparently retold to this day in Yreka's Native American community.

Patrick Croy was acquitted of murder in May 1990 on the grounds that he had killed the police officer in self-defence. However, Norma Jean Croy's conviction for aiding and abetting him still stands. In November 1991 she filed a *habeas corpus* petition, appealing for a new trial to consider the fresh evidence presented at her brother's retrial.

It has also been said that prejudice against indigenous peoples is a factor which may render them more vulnerable to torture or ill-treatment in detention. In a number of cases of torture and ill-treatment reported to Amnesty International, the perpetrators subjected indigenous peoples to racial insults as well as physical ill-treatment.

The most vulnerable victims

Certain groups of indigenous people — children, old people,

pregnant women, the mentally or physically impaired, isolated groups — are particularly vulnerable to human rights abuse.

Children

"I made out Raimundo at once. I recognized him because he was wearing red trousers. He was running towards a canoe moored at the shore. Just as Raimundo was about to reach the canoe he was hit by a bullet and fell into the river and disappeared."

At 18, Raimundo Mariano was the eldest of the six young Ticuna Indians who were among the victims of the 1988 massacre at Capacete Creek, in Brazil's Amazonas state. A total of 14 Indians were killed and another 23 were injured when settlers, allegedly hired by a timber merchant, opened fire on Indians who had gathered to protest about the theft of a bull from a Ticuna family.

Children were among those injured and killed in the attack. A 12-year-old girl, Leonita Ramos, was hit in the back and the neck, but managed to escape by running into the forest. Leila Valentin Marcos, aged six, was wounded. She was in a canoe with a number of other people, all of whom were killed. Although more than 12 pieces of gunshot had lodged in

Five-year-old Mixe Indian Misael García Santiago (right) from La Trinidad Yaveo, Oaxaca, Mexico was reportedly threatened with a gun when police officers arrested his father in January 1992.

her head, she survived by pretending to be dead. Her nine-year-old brother, Aldemir, did not.

The Ticuna are the largest of Brazil's indigenous groups, with an estimated population of 20,000. They live in the Upper Solimões region of western Brazil. The region is undergoing rapid social and economic development and the land the Indians have traditionally occupied has come under increasing threat of incursions from timber merchants, rubber tappers, landowners and fishermen, often apparently with the support of local officials. Four years after the massacre at Capacete Creek those responsible had not been brought to justice. Reported widespread local hostility to indigenous peoples has raised concern as to whether the case can be tried impartially in a local court.

Abuses against indigenous children have been reported from many other countries in the Americas. In February 1984 three plainclothes members of the Chilean security forces arrived at the home of Mapuche Germán Hueche Pañi in the Huitramealal reserve, near Temuco. Without producing any form of identification, they pulled Germán Hueche Pañi and his 16-year-old mentally handicapped son from their beds and beat them. The two were then taken to the police station in Temuco for interrogation about the supposed theft of some horses. Both were eventually released without charge.

Three children, including 10-year-old Gerónimo Soyuel Sisay, were among the 15 Tzutujil Indians killed in Guatemala in December 1990 when soldiers opened fire on a crowd of more than 2,000 unarmed indigenous peasants. Twenty-seven others, several of them children, were wounded. The Indians had gone to the military base in Sololá to denounce an earlier attack on villagers by soldiers. The government at first claimed that the December 1990 massacre had been provoked by the Indians. After widespread national and international protests at the killings, however, charges were brought against two army officers in connection with the massacre and the military agreed to move the base out of the area. In October 1991 an army sergeant was sentenced to 16 years' imprisonment for the killings. The commander of the military detachment in Panabaj was sentenced to four years' imprisonment for public intimidation and unauthorized shooting of a weapon. However, witnesses insist that those convicted were not the only soldiers who fired on the crowd.

The fate of baby María Josefa Tiu Tojín, one month old when she

© Developing World Photos

Relatives weep over the body of one of three children killed in Guatemala in 1990 when soldiers opened fire on a crowd of unarmed Tzutujil Indians. A total of 15 Indians were killed and 27 others wounded.

and her mother "disappeared", is unknown. She and her mother were among 85 Indian peasants belonging to the Communities of People in Resistance (CPR) seized by the Guatemalan military in mid-September 1990. The CPR unites indigenous communities who fled to the mountains to escape the civil conflict in Guatemala and are resisting the army's attempts to force them to back to their villages. Most of the 85 peasants were taken to an army camp and then forcibly returned to their former villages. However, according to witnesses, María Tiu Tojín was taken away for interrogation with her baby daughter and both then "disappeared". The baby's aunt, Victoria Tiu Tojín, later testified to Amnesty International that she had been threatened by members of the security forces when she tried to locate her sister and niece.

Indigenous children have been singled out because of their relationship to adults the authorities consider "dangerous" or "subversive". Melchisedec Velasco Allende and Miguel Angel Velasco, two young Triqui children from the state of Oaxaca in Mexico, are among the victims of "disappearance" whose cases Amnesty International has urged the Mexican Government to clarify. The two boys, aged 10 and 12, were allegedly abducted in July 1988 as a retaliatory measure against Miguel Angel Velasco, father of one of the boys. He had earlier received death threats from gunmen because of his activities with the Triqui organization MULT, which is actively pressing the Indians' land claim. Despite an official inquiry into the children's abduction, their whereabouts remain unknown and those responsible have not been brought to justice. The failure of the Mexican authorities to conduct effective inquiries into a series of killings and other abuses directed against the Triquis suggests that those responsible may be operating with the support or acquiescence of local officials.

The mass killings carried out by both sides in the internal armed conflict which has shaken Peru for over a decade has also counted indigenous children among its victims. Simply to be young can draw suspicion from the security forces, as young people are thought more likely to support the armed opposition. Children as young as three have "disappeared" after being detained by the security forces as suspected "subversives".

Indigenous children were also among the victims of large-scale killings by the Guatemalan military in the late 1970s and early 1980s. Testimonies collected by Amnesty International told how soldiers slit children's throats, bashed their heads against walls and disembowelled them. On several occasions, witnesses said that soldiers had explicitly singled out children.

Children have been orphaned in massive numbers through "disappearance" and extrajudicial execution. In the heavily indigenous Guatemalan department of Chimaltenango, a Guatemalan Supreme Court study conducted during 1984 and 1985 reported that some 6,500 children had lost at least one parent in recent political violence. Most of those parents were the victims of extrajudicial execution or "disappearance".

Indigenous children whose parents fled from areas of armed conflict are to be found among the thousands of abandoned, orphaned or homeless children living on the streets of several Latin American cities. Many of the children living on the streets of Guatemala City have suffered torture, "disappearance" and extrajudicial execution at the hands of the security forces. In 1990 a 17-year-old street child, Carlos Bosh, known to his friends as Gigio, "disappeared". He was one of eight members of a group of street children abducted in two separate incidents by heavily armed men in plain clothes. A 14-year-old girl was the sole known survivor. She later told Amnesty International that she and her friends were first drugged, and then taken to the Guatemala City central cemetery, where one was tied to a tree and tortured. She managed to escape. The bodies of four of her friends were found later, grotesquely mutilated. Gigio and at least one other boy remain missing. Two members of the National Police and a civilian were indicted in April 1991 in connection with the abductions and killings, but they were acquitted for "lack of evidence". The verdict has been appealed by the Public Ministry.

Street children in Guatemala City are also vulnerable to abuses by private security agents licensed to operate by the National Police and the Ministry of the Interior. On a number of occasions it has been alleged that private security agents have restrained street children, forced them to remove their clothing and set trained attack dogs on them.

Children are also heavily represented among the tens of thousands of indigenous people who have been internally displaced or forced to take refuge abroad because of human rights abuses during the civil conflict which has shaken countries like Colombia, El Salvador, Guatemala and Peru.

Women
Indigenous women as members of ethnic groups which are often

marginalized and held in low esteem by the dominant culture of their societies can be particularly vulnerable to sexual abuse, although men have also suffered such torture. Rape may occur in detention or in the context of internal conflicts where military units may be given broad powers and not held accountable for their actions. Women living in Peru's emergency zones, many of them indigenous, are alleged to have been widely subjected to rape by soldiers. According to a Yanesha Indian leader from the Peruvian lowlands quoted in the Peruvian newspaper, *Página Libre*, in July 1990: "Under the pretext of protecting us, soldiers arrive at our communities in their trucks and they take away women of all ages, saying they are suspected of terrorism, but the truth is that they rape them in their barracks, and when they get tired of them, they just dump them anywhere and they have to make their way back through the rainforest to their homes".

In 1986 legal officials told Amnesty International delegates visiting Ayacucho that rape was to be expected when troops were based in rural areas. They said it was "natural" and that prosecution could not be expected. To date, no army personnel stationed in Peru's

This woman said that her youngest child was conceived when she was raped by soldiers in the Ayacucho military zone in Peru.

emergency zones are known to have been prosecuted for rape and no effective investigations into complaints of rape by soldiers are known to have occurred. The following extracts, from a recorded testimony in the Quechua language, tells of one such raid carried out in Cangallo province: "As I knew nothing [about her husband's activities] I could not tell them anything and they hit me and threatened that if I did not tell them they would kill us and rape me. I asked, 'Why do I have to be raped?'".

The soldiers then began questioning the woman's six-year-old son, telling him his father was dead, and hitting him because he didn't know anything. The soldiers then kicked the woman in the stomach until she passed out. When she regained consciousness they were raping her. The woman's testimony continues: "I think it was the lieutenant that punched me in the stomach so that I again lost consciousness. They lifted my feet and held them between two soldiers. Then they pushed sticks into my vagina and anus.... They said ... That's what we do to terrorists".

Between February and April 1986, Peruvian troops made several incursions into Cayara, Ayacucho, in the course of which the soldiers reportedly raped at least nine women, ranging in age from

One of several Lil'Wat Indians arrested in July 1990 by the RCMP in British Columbia, in Canada. The Indians were blockading a road in protest at what they said were encroachments on their sacred lands by logging companies. Several of the Indian, including a pregnant teenager, needed medical treatment as a result of what they said was excessive force used to arrest them.

13 to 72. "[The soldiers] raped all the women in front of their children, even the old women who can scarcely walk any more", said a witness.(In many countries, indigenous women have been subjected to cruel human rights abuses, with no allowance made for those who may be pregnant or caring for small children.

In Canada, several Lil'Wat Indians, including a pregnant 17-year-old girl, required medical treatment as a result of what they said was excessive force when they were arrested in July 1990 by the RCMP at Lillooet Lake, British Columbia. The Indians were blockading a road in protest at what they said were encroachments on their sacred lands by timbering interests and hydro-electric projects, and the pollution caused by pesticides and herbicides used by the timbering companies in an effort to assure speedy reforestation.

In Brazil, five pregnant women were among an estimated 20 Pataxó-Hã-Hã-Hãe Indians from the Paragauçu-Camaruru reserve in Bahia state who needed medical treatment for the injuries they suffered when the military police tried to expel them from a ranch in southern Bahia in November 1985. The ranch was on lands designated as a Pataxó-Hã-Hã-Hãe reserve in 1926.

Women may also suffer from cruel or inhuman conditions of imprisonment when pregnant or giving birth. Like all women who are pregnant or give birth in prison in situations where medical care is inadequate or prison conditions are otherwise inhuman or degrading, indigenous women in such circumstances are at risk of miscarriage and severe injury from untreated medical complications of pregnancy, and may also bear an injured child.

In April 1990 Amnesty International called on the Mexican authorities to investigate reports that 11 members of the Tzeltal community in Chiapas had been tortured after they were detained in the context of a forced eviction of peasants from disputed land. One of the detainees who was tortured, Juliana López Gómez, was reportedly in poor health after undergoing a Caesarian section shortly before her arrest. She apparently received no medical assistance.

The elderly

> *"Approximately 70 years old, in no physical condition to flee or put up any sort of defence — he was with cowardice coldly, and barbarously murdered by the accused.... Being an 'Indian' his life was taken, 'symbolising' the clear purpose of the group to kill any Indians that they found on their way."*

This description of the killing of 70-year-old Yaminer Suruí, a leader of the isolated Suruí Indians in Brazil's Rondonia state, was given by the federal prosecutor in charge of the case.

In October 1988 the Suruí, Cinta Larga, Gavião and Arara indigenous groups became concerned at rumours that the neighbouring Zoró Indians had been persuaded to sell their lands to settlers. They considered this to be a threat not only to the Zoró, but also to their own survival. They decided to organize an expedition to persuade the Zoró not to give up their land. Some 170 Indians from the four groups entered the Zoró area, many of them armed.

According to one of the Indian party, settlers they encountered on the Zoró lands told the Indians that they would never succeed in removing them from the area and that "We will finish off the Indians". The Indians retaliated by capturing some of the settlers, stripping them, tying them up and hitting them. Although some of the Indians wanted to kill the settlers, the Zoró intervened and prevented further violence. The Indians then released their captives and set off by foot for their villages in different groups.

They were pursued by some 15 armed settlers in two jeeps, later described by the federal prosecutor as a "caravan of death". They opened fire on the first group of Indians they saw, who fled into the forest. The next group of Indians they encountered also managed to escape. Further down the road the men came across Yaminer Suruí who was returning alone to his village. This defenceless old man was shot dead by the settlers, who then quartered and burned his body.

The case was investigated by federal police. Although the police inquiry was relatively prompt, the case has failed to proceed. Four of those identified to the police as implicated in the attack were arrested and questioned. They submitted a *habeas corpus* petition but were released by a local judge before their petition was heard. Two of them are reported to have returned to the area of conflict in Rondonia, contrary to the terms of their conditional release. The first hearing of the witnesses for the prosecution was set for 15 November 1991. With considerable difficulty the Indian witnesses travelled to the hearing, but it was cancelled at the last minute. Since then there has been no further progress.

Chaqwa: abuses against refugees and the displaced

Chaqwa signifies, in the Quechua spoken in the Ayacucho area of Peru, the chaos, breakdown in order, and literal and figurative dislocation caused by the confrontation between the two diametrically opposed forces of the Peruvian army and the armed opposition PCP. In a number of countries in the Americas, including Peru, indigenous communities have become targeted for abuses by both sides during the violent disruption, the "chaqwa" of internal conflict. Many have fled the contested areas to seek protection elsewhere, sometimes within their own country, sometimes abroad.

However, even after they have fled, both those internally displaced and refugees abroad may find there is no safe haven. Often separated from their families and communities, refugees must try to build a new life in an unfamiliar cultural environment, often in a new language, and sometimes in societies where they face hostility and are at risk of abuse and deportation. The internally displaced may also have had to cross racial, cultural and linguistic barriers within their own country, and may still be under attack by their own governments or from opposition forces they have refused to support. Women and children fleeing civil conflicts during which their male relatives may have been killed often make up a disproportionate percentage of refugees and displaced people. They can be especially vulnerable to abuses of all kinds.

In 1986 Amnesty International received reports that 18 Sumo Indian refugees fleeing internal conflict in Nicaragua had been abducted from the camp in southern Honduras where they had sought refuge. They had reportedly been seized by the *Contra*, who were operating from bases in Honduras with the collusion of the Honduran military authorities and the backing of the US Government. The *Contra* apparently intended to compel the Indians to join their ranks. Amnesty International issued urgent appeals to the Honduran authorities to ensure the physical safety of the Indians reported abducted. A commission established by the Honduran armed forces to investigate the incident located the unit responsible for the abductions some four months later, and was able to interview 12 of those who had been abducted. Although they said they had not been kidnapped, the Nicaraguan Association for Human Rights (ANPDH) considered that they had clearly been recruited under psychological pressure; some were under 16 years of age. ANPDH eventually secured information about the whereabouts of the remaining six Sumo refugees; four were described as fighting of their own free will; two had apparently returned to their villages along the border.

At the height of the army counter-insurgency in Guatemala in the late 1970s and early 1980s tens of thousands of indigenous people from Guatemala sought refuge abroad. In Mexico, they remained vulnerable to cross-border raids carried out by the Guatemalan military and civil patrols working under army command. In 1984 an Amnesty International delegation interviewed survivors of an attack by Guatemalan forces on the Chupadero refugee camp in southern Mexico. One of the survivors had been shot through the eye; he died shortly afterwards of his wounds. On a number of occasions, it was alleged that Mexican security forces cooperated with their Guatemalan counterparts in carrying out such raids or in directing abuses against both Mexican aid workers and the refugees themselves.

Guatemalans displaced within their own country during the civil conflict remained in jeopardy in the cities where they sought refuge. Amnesty International has recorded scores of abuses directed against indigenous peasants who had fled to Guatemala City. According to testimonies collected by the organization from the displaced and those assisting them, the Guatemalan army regularly brought local civil defence patrol members and others from areas believed to have been sympathetic to the armed opposition to urban centres where displaced people were known to congregate. It was reported that some of those brought to identify "subversives" were hooded or masked and appeared to have burns on their hands suggesting they had been tortured to force them to collaborate with the army. Some of the people identified as "subversives" later "disappeared". Others were taken back to their villages and threatened with torture and death unless they identified other "subversives".

As the civil conflict raged in Guatemala, the US Government rejected thousands of applications for asylum from those fleeing governments it was supporting in Central America. Those refused included Guatemalan indigenous people. Amnesty International repeatedly appealed to the US Government not to return refugees to their countries of origin, where they were at risk of arbitrary arrest, torture, "disappearance" or extrajudicial execution.

Isolated Indians
In several countries in Latin America, there are a number of isolated groups which have had little or no contact with non-indigenous society, or who have come into contact with it only recently. They are particularly vulnerable to abuse of their rights and are often unable to make representations to the central auth-

orities in an effort to protect their lands and rights, as they do not speak the language of the majority culture, and have no understanding of the legal, social and political mechanisms of the surrounding society.

Reports of abuses against isolated Indians by members of the security forces, private agencies seeking to exploit their traditional lands, who operate with official complicity or acquiescence, or by members of missionary groups to whom the state has granted wide-ranging authority have been received from a number of countries including Paraguay and Bolivia.

Abuses against isolated Indians have been best documented in Brazil, where 87 indigenous groups are estimated to have become extinct between 1900 and 1957. Some were destroyed by disease and starvation, often related to loss of their lands or pollution of their environment by mining and other commercial exploitation. Other groups were eliminated by killings carried out by miners, settlers and timber interests moving into their areas. The government's failure to protect the Indians and to prosecute those responsible for attacks on them suggests official acquiescence in the abuses against them. In some cases, the direct complicity of local authorities in the killing or "disappearance" of Brazilian Indians has been documented. Although Brazilian Indians are afforded extensive protection in law, in practice there has been a pattern whereby the authorities have been ineffectual in guaranteeing their rights or investigating abuses committed against them by non-state agents acting on some occasions, it is alleged, with the complicity or acquiescence of local officials.

Formally, it is now Brazilian policy to locate isolated groups of Indians and protect them from incursions which could result in abuses against them, but Amnesty International has received reporrts from several sources, including officials of the National Indian Foundation (FUNAI), the government body responsible for indigenous affairs, that this policy is not always implemented in practice.

The Korubu are one of six groups of isolated Indians living in the Javari Valley of Amazonas State in northwest Brazil. They are much feared by the non-indigenous population, though rarely seen by them.

Commercial logging and fishing in the Korubu area has disturbed their habitat, and provoked reprisals by them against settlers. A 1985 FUNAI injunction, barring members of the non-indigenous population from entering the area, has not been enforced. As early as 1987 local FUNAI staff warned, in a report to their regional headquarters, that the Korubus were in danger from the non-indigenous population and called for measures to protect them: "If FUNAI doesn't take energetic measures, it is possible to foresee the unleashing of a war against the Indians, which would be a catastrophe, bearing in mind that they are not in any way prepared to meet this threat".

In September 1989 three Korubu Indians were ambushed and killed on the banks of the Itui River by settlers. According to testimonies given to the police, three Korubus had appeared at the river bank, at the settlement known as Gamboa, the previous evening and stood and observed a football game being played by some of the settlers. Members of Indigenous Coordination of the Javari Valley, an independent indigenous organization, believe the three Korubus may have been trying to make contact with the settlers. According to testimony later taken in a police inquiry into the killings, the villagers became frightened at the approach of the Korubus and called a meeting to decide what to do. They were joined by several fishermen from the nearby town of Benjamin Constant who allegedly urged them to mount a hunting party. According to the testimony of the participants, the fishermen and villagers ambushed the three Indians the next day, killed them and buried their bodies.

News of the killings might never have reached the public were it not for the actions of a local priest, Father Joseney Lira. After hearing rumours that three Indians had been killed he visited Gamboa the following month, was told of the incident by settlers, and informed the press. As a result of the publicity the Attorney General ordered the federal police to investigate the case. Local FUNAI staff had apparently known of the incident but had taken no action on the grounds that it was impossible to investigate such cases. A town councillor from Benjamin Constant also knew of the incident, having reportedly been presented with clubs belonging to the murdered Indians, but did nothing.

Some two months after the killings federal police officers and FUNAI staff retrieved the bodies of the three Indians, which had been buried in the river bank. They then took testimonies from settlers, some of whom had been directly involved in the killings. Some of those interviewed had expressed surprise to find that their Indian victims were "just like us". The federal police inquiry was completed in July 1990 and recommended charging six people with the killings. The conclusions of the inquiry appear to contradict statements taken in November 1989 from alleged participants in which they admitted holding a meeting in which it was decided to track and kill the Korubus. The inquiry report describes the killings almost as if they had happened by accident.

In a further unexplained development, the case was passed to the jurisdiction of the state courts. The killings had occurred within a recognized Indian area and theoretically therefore fell within federal jurisdiction.

It was more than six months before the local state prosecutor filed charges against the accused. The case apparently collapsed in June 1991, when the court suspended proceedings indefinitely, claiming it did not have the resources to summon the accused for trial.

3

Protection for indigenous peoples: theory and practice

Protected by law

In common with each and every one of the world's citizens, the fundamental human rights of indigenous people are protected by international law. These include: the right to life; the right to freedom from torture and other cruel, inhuman or degrading treatment or punishment; the right to freedom of thought, conscience and religion. These fundamental human rights must be upheld whatever the circumstances. No exceptions are permitted: neither a threat of war or a state of war, nor internal political instability, nor any public emergency. These and numerous other rights, many of which fall outside Amnesty International's scope for action, are set forth in international and regional treaties and declarations[2].

Governments are obliged to uphold human rights and to provide redress for the victims of violations. They must carry out full investigations, bring the perpetrators to justice and provide compensation for victims and their relatives. Even when the violations occurred under a previous government, international law says that its successors inherit these obligations — a principle reaffirmed in 1988 by the Inter-American Court of Human Rights.

However, the scant regard (if not outright disregard) many governments have often paid to these obligations, resulting in some cases in the near extinction of indigenous populations, has led to a search for extra means of protecting them.

In 1971 the Inter-American Commission on Human Rights (IACHR) of the OAS considered that "special protection for indigenous populations constitutes a sacred commitment of the [member] states" and recommended that governments take steps to protect indigenous peoples against abuses by state agents, stating that "indigenous persons ... should not be the object of discrimination of any kind". In October 1988 the UN Programme for Action for the Second Decade of the Fight Against Racism and Racial Discrimination organized a global consultation to coordinate international activities against racism and racial discrimination, which suggested that governments adopt legislative, administrative, economic and social measures to eradicate policies and practices of discrimination, recognizing the vulnerability of indigenous populations[3].

International efforts to protect human rights

Since the early 1970s the UN has been involved in several initiatives aimed at developing specific standards concerning the rights of indigenous peoples, and, with the ILO and the OAS, has taken initiatives designed to protect the broadest rights of indigenous peoples.

The UN Working Group on Indigenous Populations, established in 1982 as part of the UN Sub-Commission on Prevention of Discrimination and Protection of Minorities, meets annually to monitor the promotion and protection of human rights and fundamental freedoms of indigenous peoples. The Working Group was instructed to give special attention to the evolution of standards concerning the rights of indigenous peoples. In addition to its work on standard setting, the Working Group has also carried out a number of missions to investigate the situation of specific indigenous groups, including the Yanomami of Brazil.

Organizations and individuals representing indigenous communities, and independent scholars with expertise in indigenous rights, may attend the Working Group's meetings, and participate in the debate along with the Working Group members, other non-governmental organizations, and government representatives. Participants in the meetings may present information about human rights violations against indigenous peoples.

In 1985 the Working Group began to develop a Declaration on Indigenous Rights. The draft declaration contains provisions devoted to protecting rights. These include: collective cultural and ethnic rights; rights to land and resources; economic and social rights, including the maintenance of traditional economic structures and ways of life; civil and political rights, including respect for indigenous laws and customs; participation in decision-making in all matters affecting their lives and destiny; and the collective right to autonomy. The draft declaration also contains recommendations for fair procedures for resolving conflicts of disputes between states and indigenous peoples.

Extensive studies have been undertaken by Special Rapporteurs of the UN Sub-Commission on Prevention of Discrimination and Protection of Minorities, in the areas of self-determination and minorities, as well as on indigenous populations specifically. A current study is investigating the links between human rights and environmental concerns. The UN Centre on Transnational Corporations' study on the effects of transnational investments and operations on indigenous lands has evaluated issues which could have bearing, for example, on political and legal procedures to guarantee indigenous peoples their intellectual rights; protection of their homelands from ecologically unsound exploitation; application of traditional medicine; the transfer of agricultural and forestry management technologies; and the development of alternative products from the forest.

In June 1992 the UN brought together heads of state and government from around the world to meet in Rio de Janeiro, Brazil for the United Nations Conference on Environment and Development (UNCED). The primary purpose of the conference was to move environment issues into the centre of the development agenda and of economic policy making. A large number of development, environmental and indigenous groups contributed to UNCED Working Groups and Preparatory Committees, and concurrent with the official UNCED activities, met independently to examine linkages between development, environmental, indigenous and other human rights issues.

The UN has designated 1993 as International Year for the World's Indigenous People aimed at strengthening international cooperation for the solution of problems faced by indigenous communities in such areas as human rights, the environment, development, education and health. The UN's World Conference on Human Rights, also scheduled for 1993, is to examine, among other things, the relationship between development and the enjoyment of economic, social and cultural rights as well as civil and political rights, and can be expected to deal with issues of importance to indigenous peoples.

The ILO, a specialized UN agency, has studied the plight of indigenous peoples since it was founded; it undertook studies of the conditions of indigenous workers as early as 1921. In 1957 the ILO drew up the Indigenous and Tribal Peoples Convention,

No. 107, which aimed at the protection of indigenous peoples and their integration and assimilation into national societies. Twenty-eight countries, 15 of them in the Americas, ratified Convention 107, thereby undertaking to provide regular reports to the ILO on the situation of indigenous people in their country and on national law and practice in regard to them.

Since the Convention was drafted some three decades ago, thinking among both intergovernmental agencies and indigenous peoples themselves altered as to the notion and desirability of integration, leading the ILO to revise the Convention. The new Convention, Indigenous and Tribal Peoples Convention No. 169 (1989), is based on the assumption that indigenous peoples should remain distinct elements within national societies. In addition, Article 18 of the new convention stipulates that "Adequate penalties shall be established by law for unauthorized intrusion upon, or use of, the lands of the peoples concerned, and governments shall take measures to prevent such offenses". At the time of writing, three governments in the Americas had ratified the new Convention, which came into force in September 1991.

Elements of the new Convention which relate specifically to those rights within the scope of Amnesty International's work include: provisions on the protection of physical integrity; enjoyment of human rights and fundamental freedoms without hindrance or discrimination; penalties before the law in accordance with internationally recognized human rights; special safeguards against abuse of indigenous peoples' rights; and the rights to freedom of association and lawful trade union activities.

In 1989 the OAS took steps to adopt a regional instrument to protect indigenous peoples. The General Assembly of the OAS resolved to mandate the IACHR and the Inter-American Indian Institute to prepare a juridical instrument on the rights of indigenous peoples. The IACHR has now approved a methodology for the preparation of the proposed new instrument; it expects to forward a Preliminary Draft to the Permanent Council and General Assembly of the OAS in 1994.

The OAS has been active in developing programs and administrative structures on behalf of the indigenous peoples of the Americas. Various OAS bodies have affirmed important principles, such as self-determination and equality, in their programs of action. The OAS has chartered a special body, the Inter-American Indian Institute, to promote indigenous issues, including fostering an appreciation for indigenous knowledge. Other agencies of the inter-American system, such as the IACHR and Inter-American Court of Human Rights, have dealt with human rights matters of concern to indigenous peoples. The IACHR has, for example, examined allegations of human rights violations against the Aché-guayakí of Paraguay, the Yanomami of Brazil, the Miskitos of Nicaragua and the Guahibo of Colombia. In the context of its inquiries into violations against Guatemalan and Peruvian peasants the IACHR has studied the massive violations suffered by indigenous peoples in those countries.

The impact of uncontrolled development projects on areas traditionally occupied by indigenous peoples, and on indigenous peoples themselves, has been a subject of great attention throughout the Americas. The World Bank has adopted a pioneering written policy setting out criteria for the selection and monitoring of such projects. The policy states that the Bank will provide assistance for development projects in areas being used or occupied by tribal peoples only if such projects include adequate measures to safeguard the integrity and well-being of those concerned and it is satisfied that the borrowing government or agency supports and can implement such measures effectively.

The national picture
Until recently many countries in the Americas have generally maintained that there is no need for special legislation to protect the rights of minorities and that protection of general human rights on a non-discriminatory basis was sufficient. However, this is clearly not enough. The ICCPR, for example, explicitly refers to the need to protect the rights of national minorities to enjoy their own culture, practice their own religion and use their own language.

Steps have also been taken in some American countries to acknowledge the importance of promoting and protecting the practices, customs and values of indigenous communities. Such customs and practices, often referred to as indigenous "customary law", cover such matters as: internal order and general standards for public behaviour within the community; the rights and obligations of its members; definition and classification of crimes; sanctions for criminal behaviour; procedures to deal with conflicts and disputes; definition of responsibilities and functions of public authorities. However, conflicts continue to arise between national law and indigenous "customary law", often with regard to land and resource use and ownership, and can lead to human rights violations of concern to Amnesty International.

Legislation on indigenous affairs differs significantly between countries in the region. In some states, there is little or no difference between the treatment under national law of indigenous peoples and that of the non-indigenous peasantry and rural labour force as regards systems of ownership and use of land. In others, often those where a smaller percentage of the population is defined as indigenous, the ownership and tenure of indigenous land has at times been regulated by special protective legislation, which usually includes provisions against the seizure of such land.

In many countries in the Americas, the gap between the rights and protection promised indigenous peoples and reality are marked. In North America, for example, guarantees of equality and non-discrimination are incorporated into constitutional law as well as into legislation governing Indian affairs, but are not always applied or enforced. Thus, the Canadian Charter of Rights and Freedoms[4] provides detailed guarantees regarding non-discrimination. Nevertheless, several official studies found that general prejudice against Native Canadians led to discrimination in the criminal justice systems of some provinces.

© Luis Donisete Benzi Grupioni/Arquivo Commissão Pro-Indio

When the 1988 Constitution of Brazil was being drafted Indian groups lobbied the Constituent Assembly. The constitution is considered one of the most advanced in the world in the extent to which it protects Indian rights. However, it is often when Indian groups attempt to exercise the rights guaranteed them by the constitution that they suffer abuses.

Official policy in relation to indigenous groups in the USA covers American Indians, Native Alaskans and Native Hawaiians. With respect to American Indian groups the policy has ranged from initial recognition of independent status, to forced relocation and actions which resulted in massive violations including extra-judicial executions, to assimilation and, in recent years, to programs presented as aiming to foster tribal self-determination and economic development.

Violating human rights with impunity

"In no circumstances, including a state of war, siege or other public emergency, shall blanket immunity from prosecution be granted to any person allegedly involved in extra-legal, arbitrary or summary executions".

UN Principles on the Effective Prevention and Investigation of Extra-legal, Arbitrary and Summary Executions, adopted by the UN Economic and Social Council in May 1989.

Human rights violations by state agents are seldom effectively investigated; cases in which members of the security forces guilty of the killing, torture and "disappearance" of indigenous peoples have been brought to justice are rare. This tacit protection from prosecution has often been extended beyond the ranks of official state agents, to include members of "death squads", hired gunmen in the pay of powerful local interests, civilian vigilantes and armed settlers. It is a phenomenon known as impunity and it is in evidence throughout the region, whether the victims are Indians, or peasants or human rights activists.

Amnesty International believes that the phenomenon of impunity is one of the key factors contributing to the pattern of human rights violations against indigenous people in the Americas. Impunity, literally the exemption from punishment, has serious implications for the proper administration of justice. International standards clearly require states to undertake proper investigations into human rights violations and to ensure that those responsible are brought to justice. The adequate investigation of human rights abuses is essential if the full truth is to emerge. Victims, their relatives and the society at large all have a vital interest in knowing the truth about past abuses.

Similarly, bringing the perpetrators to justice is not only important in respect of the individual case, but also sends a clear message that violations of human rights will not be tolerated and that those who commit such acts will be held fully accountable. When investigations are not pursued and the perpetrators are not held to account, a self-perpetuating cycle of violence is set in motion resulting in continuing violations of human rights cloaked by impunity.

Even when investigations are carried out and judicial proceedings are brought against the perpetrators, the institutions responsible for the administration of justice are often weak or inefficient and may be susceptible to pressure from other state authorities or by the perpetrators. This may be particularly the case when indigenous peoples are the victims, because of their position in society and remoteness of the areas in which some of them live. Extraordinary measures may also contribute to subverting the process of justice, such as the transfer of such cases to special tribunals, often military, as has occurred in Peru and Colombia.

In some countries those responsible for human rights violations against indigenous peoples have been officially placed beyond the reach of the law. The civilian government which took office in Guatemala in 1986 inherited an amnesty law from its military predecessors which exonerated all those responsible for human rights violations in the previous four years. In 1985, shortly before he took office, the new civilian president had announced: "We are not going to be able to investigate the past. We would have to put the entire army in jail". Justice was thereby denied to the thousands of indigenous victims killed, abducted, raped and tortured by the Guatemalan army. In subsequent years, in only a few cases have proceedings been initiated against security force agents, usually police officers, for human rights violations. Where convictions have been gained, they have customarily been overturned on technicalities or because of military or police pressure. In 1988, for example, six National Police officers were found guilty of the kidnapping and murder of two agronomy students, one of them of indigenous origin, whose tortured bodies were found days after witnesses saw them being seized by heavily armed men in plain clothes. An investigation assisted by the US FBI had found strong evidence, some of it developed through forensic techniques, to link the police officers to the crime. Laboratory testing of hair samples taken from the police chief's car indicated that at some point after their capture, the victims had been held in that vehicle. Nonetheless, the kidnapping conviction was overturned on appeal, and after another appeal, the police officers were freed in 1990, on the grounds that there was not enough evidence to substantiate the murder charges. The relatives of the two murdered agronomists have told Amnesty International that they have received death threats from the freed police officers on several occasions, and now fear for their lives. They also say that to dissuade the family from further pursuing the case, the police officers have put pressure on local employers and family members have lost their jobs.

After Chile returned to democratic government in 1990, a National Commission of Truth and Reconciliation (CNVR) was appointed to look into serious human rights violations committed during Chile's years of military government. The CNVR identified the cases of nearly 100 Mapuche Indians who were executed or who "disappeared" following their abduction by the army or security forces. (There are believed to have been other Mapuche Indians who "disappeared", but their families are said to still be too afraid to come forward or have not given testimony because they live in isolated communities or do not speak Spanish.) However, those responsible are protected from prosecution by an amnesty law passed in Chile in 1978. The amnesty covers all those who were the "authors, accomplices or accessories" of crimes committed in Chile between 11 September 1973 and 10 March 1978. This law continues to be used to close investigations into abuses which occurred before 1978 before the full facts have been clarified and criminal responsibility established.

The events which followed the 1988 massacre of some 30 Indian peasants at Cayara in Peru's Ayacucho province were described by a Lima newspaper as "an anthology of impunity". The massacre was apparently in reprisal for the ambush of a military convoy by the PCP armed opposition group the previous day in which three soldiers were killed and 15 others wounded. The presumption that entire communities may be considered collectively responsible for PCP actions has often been invoked in justification of what amounts to a policy of indiscriminate killing and "disappearance".

Despite an exceptionally thorough investigation, which concluded that the security forces were responsible, no one has been brought to justice. A public prosecutor travelled to the area and, with the aid of an interpreter, took testimonies from the Quechua-speaking witnesses and victims' relatives. The prosecutor summarized the testimony of an 11-year-old boy who witnessed his father's extrajudicial execution as follows: "Soldiers wearing black

Top: Mapuche Indian Pedro Millalén Huechuñir, a farmworker, was 35 years old when he "disappeared" after being abducted by the Chilean police in September 1973. Below: Bernardo Nahuelcoi Chihuaicura (pictured with his family), a 32-year-old Mapuche Indian, was extrajudicially executed in Chile in October 1973.

ski masks, armed with heavy weapons ... made his father lie on the ground ... one kicked him while another hit him with the butt of a gun. He clung to his father and told the soldiers that his father was innocent, but the soldiers frightened him away with a cattle whip ... he didn't see his father again. Later, the soldiers told him to get away and he ran, along with the women, one of whom told him they had cut off his father's head".

Two of the main witnesses who had testified to the special prosecutor, Fernandina Palomino Quispe and Justiniano Tinco García, were killed in December 1988. They were travelling in a truck with several other people when they were stopped at a road block by an army patrol in Toccto. The two were singled out, taken from the truck, beaten and slashed with knives before being deliberately killed in full view of the other passengers. Their deaths brought to eight the number of those who had given testimony concerning the Cayara killings and had subsequently been extrajudicially executed or "disappeared". A ninth witness was killed in September 1989. Marta Crisóstomo García, a 22-year-old nurse, had moved from Cayara to the Ayacucho town of Huamanga after receiving threats. On the morning of 8 September, a squad of hooded men in army uniform broke into her home and shot her dead. The prosecutor who had first investigated the case left the country in November 1989 after receiving threats.

In February 1992 the IACHR found, with respect to the Cayara massacre, that a number of rights protected under the American Convention on Human Rights had been violated by the Peruvian army. It referred the case to the Inter-American Court of Human Rights.

The Zenú Indians of the San Andrés de Sotavento district of Córdoba in Colombia have been involved in a long-standing dispute with local landowners over land which the Indians claim is an indigenous reserve. Under Colombian law, indigenous land cannot be sold or transferred outside the Indian communities. In October 1986 the Zenú community was raided by some 20 police officers, reportedly accompanied by a local landowner and his lawyer. Eleven Indians were detained and 20 hectares of their crops and some of their homes were reportedly destroyed with the use of the landowner's tractors. The following day, four police officers, again accompanied by the landowner and his lawyer,

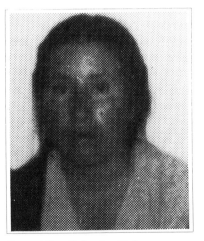

Fernandina Palomino Quispe was one of the witnesses to the massacre of over 30 indigenous peasants in Cayara, Peru. She was killed by soldiers a few months after this photograph was taken. Nine witnesses to the Cayara massacre have been extrajudicially executed.

returned to the Zenú community and arrested Pedro Hernández, a community leader. They later denied that he had been detained. His body was found two days after his arrest. He appeared to have been tortured and there were bullet wounds in his head. To Amnesty International's knowledge no one has been brought to trial for the killing of Pedro Hernández. Since then many other leaders and members of the Zenú community have been killed or "disappeared" with the apparent complicity of the Colombian police and army. No one has yet been brought to justice.

Governments rarely admit that their own agents have been responsible for human rights violations even in the face of overwhelming evidence, including medical documentation. When compelled to admit that it has happened, they will usually insist that it does not represent official policy, but was carried out by individual security agents or units acting unofficially. Even when the authorities have admitted that state agents were responsible for human rights violations, steps are rarely taken to discipline or punish those responsible.

Amnesty International has documented hundreds of complaints of torture in Mexico; many indigenous leaders involved in land rights struggles have been among the victims. Often, torture has been used to force them to confess to criminal offences. Amnesty International has repeatedly called upon the Mexican authorities to bring perpetrators of torture to justice and to take steps to bring an end to the practice. In September 1991, Amnesty International published *Torture with Impunity*, which documented torture throughout Mexico. The report was based on scores of interviews with victims and witnesses collected by Amnesty International as well as other national and international human rights monitors. In some cases, Amnesty International medical personnel had been able to examine victims and confirm that they exhibited signs of torture consistent with that they described suffering at the hands of Mexican security personnel. Nonetheless, despite the mass of information suggesting that torture in Mexico continues to be widespread, Mexican officials reacted to this report by claiming that the incidence of torture was diminishing and that it now occurs only in isolated cases. Officials also pointed to new legislation intended, they said, to end torture in Mexico, and declared that a number of federal police officials had been dismissed for committing abuses, and that 39 had been prosecuted. However, it later became known that most of the sanctions against officials referred to were apparently not related to human rights abuses, but were for offences such as drug trafficking and corruption.

In only one case known to Amnesty International have those responsible for killing Indians in Brazil been brought to justice. In 1988 two gunmen, a landowner and a timber merchant were given sentences ranging from two to 27 years' imprisonment for the murder of three Xacriabá Indians in Minas Gerais state. Two of the Indians, Rosalindo Gomes de Oliveira and José Pereria dos Santos, were shot as they slept. The third, Manoel Fiusa da Silva, was killed as he ran to their assistance. This is the only case involving the killing of Indians to have been tried and convicted in a federal court.

Brazil's 1988 Constitution provides for the intervention of the Federal Attorney General's Office in all cases involving Indians. Indigenous groups have welcomed this provision, as the pattern in Brazil is that many abuses against indigenous peoples are carried out with impunity by non-state agents, and they consider that such cases are more likely to see progress in federal courts, given the reported susceptibility of state courts to local political pressure hostile to the Indians. However, in the few cases in Brazil where proceedings have been initiated local or state courts have not transferred jurisdiction to federal courts and the cases have languished in local courts for years without resolution, apparently due to pressures from hostile local settlers and officials. The most extreme example known to Amnesty International of the inordinate delays in proceedings against those responsible for abuses against Indians in Brazil stemmed from the 1963 killing of 31 Ureu-wau-wau Indians, and the abduction of 28 women and children from the same group. The Ureu-wau-wau of Rondonia state are a nomadic hunter-gatherer people who have suffered abuses as private interests, seeking to exploit resources, have moved onto their traditional lands. Some 30 years after the killings, the case has still not been transferred to federal jurisdiction; the rubber estate owner charged with the murders is now too old under Brazilian legislation to be imprisoned.

Triqui Indians living in isolated settlements in Oaxaca, Mexico, many of whom speak little or no Spanish, have been frequent victims of abuses, including torture and killings. Many of the victims were community leaders who had taken a strong stand on political and economic issues, asserting claims for what they maintained were their communal lands reportedly usurped by owners of private estates and local authorities. In the late 1970s and early 1980s abuses were allegedly carried out by soldiers stationed in the area, acting in collaboration with the municipal authorities. Between July 1976 and December 1982, 37 Triquis, including a number of MULT leaders, were murdered in separate incidents; 18 more are known to have been killed by gunmen between February 1989 and September 1990. The failure of the Mexican authorities to conduct investigations into the killings and other abuses against the Triqui contributes to a widely held belief that the gunmen are carrying out their activities with the support or acquiescence of local government officials. Amnesty International knows of no instance in which those responsible for abuses against the Triqui Indians have been brought to justice.

4

Campaigning for indigenous rights

The widespread human rights violations suffered by indigenous peoples of the Americas remain of deep and grave concern. At the same time, indigenous peoples and their supporters are increasing their campaign for indigenous rights and the renovation of indigenous societies.

Because governments often do not protect indigenous rights, and because indigenous peoples may not accept central government jurisdiction over their affairs, indigenous peoples of the Americas have increasingly come together to demand respect for their rights. In the past 20 years, hundreds of new indigenous organizations have joined already existing groups in the campaign to protect indigenous rights. Some work at community level, some, like the Mayan Institute in Belize, have an ethnic base, while others are multi-ethnic or international. National indigenous organizations have been formed in almost every country in the Americas. In addition to indigenous groups, a wide range of non-governmental organizations and church groups are also active in researching, publicizing, advocating and supporting action on indigenous affairs.

The issues on which indigenous people are campaigning include: the defence of civil and political rights; the struggle for land and resources; more and better state services; bilingual education and the defence of their cultural heritage; the incorporation of indigenous peoples into national political life and their representation on government bodies that affect their interests.

Many of the indigenous groups campaigning on these and other issues have made progress in placing their concerns on the agendas of their national legislatures. They have raised public awareness of the discrimination and repression they have suffered, and of their aims and aspirations. In some countries indigenous political parties exist; in others indigenous people have been elected to their national legislatures. Many of the activists involved in organizing indigenous peoples and publicizing their grievances and objectives have been victimised. But this has not stopped the work for which some of them have given their lives.

Victimizing the activists

Indigenous people campaigning on issues of concern to them — such as protection, retention, return or just compensation for land to which they claim traditional rights; self-determination or autonomy; environmental protection; or defence of cultural or other rights — have frequently themselves become victims of human rights violations. They are often singled out because of their leadership role within their communities or their opposition to government policies.

In Chile, a program of agrarian reform implemented by the Allende government had enabled some Mapuches to regain some of the lands taken from them since the arrival of the Spanish in the 16th century. After the military coup in 1973 which overthrew the Allende government, many Mapuche leaders, activists and community members were arrested and tortured. Others were killed or "disappeared". The fate of more than 100 is unknown. Much of the land that the Mapuche had legally recovered was once again lost to them.

"On the day of the coup, the big landowners, the land barons, the military and the *carabineros* [uniformed police] started a great manhunt against the Mapuches who had struggled and gained their land back..." Thus the UN Ad Hoc Working Group on the Situation of Human Rights in Chile described, in 1978, the beginning of wholesale abuses against the largest of Chile's indigenous groups, the Mapuche Indians. A 1980 Inter-Church Committee on Human Rights in Latin America report described how the Mapuche had been "pursued ... and hunted like animals ... simply because they were Indians". The Mapuche are estimated to number between 600,000 and one million; some are based in the rural areas, others now live in towns.

During the 1980s, Amnesty International campaigned on behalf of a number of Mapuche activists who were subjected to short-term

Kaiowá Indian leader Marçal Tupa-y de Souza Guarani was chosen to represent indigenous peoples when Pope John Paul II visited Brazil in 1980, in a special appeal to draw public attention to attacks on Brazilian Indians and their land. He was killed in 1983 in unclarified circumstances. At the time he was campaigning for the demarcation of Kaiowá lands, which was disputed by local ranchers. No one has been brought to justice for his murder.

Four women in Ayacucho hold photographs of relatives who have "disappeared". In Peru, women like these often go to extraordinary lengths to discover the fate of "disappeared" relatives. As a result, they may themselves become the victims of human rights violations.

81

arbitrary detention, banishment to remote areas of the country, and harassment as a result of their activities. José Santos Millao Palacios, for example, was detained on several occasions because of his leading role in AD-MAPU, an organization which works for Mapuche rights, and was banished on two occasions, for periods of three months. Amnesty International campaigned for his immediate and unconditional release on the grounds that he had been detained and banished merely because of his non-violent AD-MAUP activities.

In Brazil, in 1988 two Kaiapó Indians were prosecuted under the Foreigners Law for having "contributed to a crime" allegedly committed by a North American ethnobotanist. The three had attended a seminar in the USA where they had expressed concerns regarding a proposed hydro-electric project which would flood officially recognized indigenous territory. Brazilian officials apparently believed that the Indians' comments had delayed a World Bank loan to Brazil for the project. When one of the Indians went to testify to the federal court about the case, the federal judge refused to hear his testimony because the Indian was wearing traditional dress, rather than the shirt and trousers demanded by the judge. The charges were later dropped.

Since the Indian protest movement began in Ecuador in June 1990, there have been reports that heavily armed paramilitary groups, some of them apparently acting with official acquiescence or the direct cooperation of local official forces, have been responsible for abuses against Indians, particularly in areas where indigenous groups have been involved in land disputes. To Amnesty International's knowledge, no member of the paramilitary groups operating in Ecuador has ever been convicted of abuses against indigenous peoples.

Indigenous community leaders in Ecuador appear to have been particularly singled out as targets of abuses including harassment, torture (including rape) and killing. One victim was Quechua-speaker Julio Cabascango, human rights officer of an Imbabura indigenous peasant federation. He was stabbed to death in March 1990 in Huaycopungo, Imbabura, apparently by men in the pay of a local landowner. Two men allegedly directly involved in his murder were arrested, but were said to have escaped. To Amnesty International's knowledge they are still at large.

Several indigenous leaders in Ecuador were detained, tortured and ill-treated in reprisal for demonstrations organized in June 1991 calling, among other things, for an investigation into Julio

Cabascango's death and for the resolution of land disputes in highland indigenous regions. A cousin of the murdered man, 27-year-old Quechua-speaker José María Cabascango, was arrested by the army with other indigenous leaders as they visited local communities participating in a two-day protest. The protest consisted of a series of peaceful activities, including road blockades, organized by groups throughout the country to call attention to indigenous demands.

José María Cabascango was reportedly subjected to racial insults during the arrest. He was transferred to the custody of the Ecuadorian investigative police (SIC). He later alleged he was hung by his thumbs and subjected to blows to the ears, mock execution and death threats while in SIC custody. The SIC was disbanded following a presidential decree of September 1991. This was prompted by the findings of the government-appointed commission which investigated the "disappearance" of two teenage brothers. The commission found that the SIC had been responsible for their "disappearance" and had systematically engaged in "torture, arbitrary detention and the use of cruel, inhuman and degrading treatment". The authorities announced

Above: Julio Cabascango, human rights officer of an indigenous peasant federation in the province of Imbabura, Ecuador, was stabbed to death in March 1990. His killers were reportedly employed by a local landowner. Below: José María Cabascango, Quechua-speaking human rights secretary of the Confederation of Indigenous Nationalities of Ecuador, was allegedly tortured by the Ecuadorian investigative police in June 1991.

that a judicial police force would replace the SIC.

Whole communities of Indians in Ecuador have been the victims of combined operations involving armed plainclothes groups and the army or police. For example, villagers involved in a land dispute in Huaycopungo have been attacked several times by paramilitary forces. In November 1990 Amnesty International called on the Ecuadorian authorities to investigate reports that on 9 November some 50 uniformed police, accompanied by civilians believed to be working for local landowners, had entered the community of Huaycopungo, and opened fire on residents. At least three members of the community were shot and wounded. In January 1991 four children were reportedly wounded when paramilitaries attacked Huaycopungo's Sunday school.

In the USA, Native Americans campaigning for protection of traditional Indian lands and resources have sometimes been involved in violent confrontations with the authorities. Lakota Sioux Leonard Peltier, a leader of the American Indian Movement (AIM), is currently serving two consecutive life sentences for killing two FBI agents on the Pine Ridge Indian Reservation, South Dakota, in 1975. The agents were shot and

©*Leonard Peltier Defense Committee*

AIM leader Leonard Peltier is serving two life sentences for the murder of FBI agents on Pine Ridge Indian Reservation, South Dakota, USA. During his trial, the FBI withheld evidence which might have assisted his defence. Amnesty International believes he should be granted a retrial.

killed at point-blank range after being wounded in a gunfight with Indian activists in which a Native American also died.

Amnesty International has repeatedly expressed its concern about certain irregularities in the proceedings which led to Leonard Peltier's conviction. Before he stood trial, Leonard Peltier was extradited from Canada on the basis of evidence which the FBI admitted fabricating. The trial judge refused to allow Leonard Peltier's lawyers to introduce evidence of FBI misconduct in other cases. The defence considered such evidence would have shown the jury that the authorities were prepared to use improper methods, including coercion of witnesses, to secure convictions in particular cases. Since the trial, it has emerged that evidence which might have assisted Leonard Peltier's case was withheld from the court by the prosecution. This evidence included a 1975 telex from a FBI ballistics expert in which it was stated that the gun allegedly belonging to Leonard Peltier had a "different firing pin" to the gun used in the killings. At a court hearing in 1984, another FBI expert testified that the telex had been a progress report and that a bullet casing, which the prosecution claimed had been fired at point-blank range and had not been tested before the telex was sent, was later found to match "positively" with Leonard Peltier's gun. An appeal court found that the prosecution had withheld evidence which would have been favourable to Leonard Peltier, but considered that this evidence would not have materially affected the outcome of the trial.

Amnesty International has also expressed concern that Leonard Peltier may have been aggressively prosecuted on criminal charges by the FBI because of his role in AIM and that his extradition to the USA from Canada in 1976 to stand trial was granted on the basis of evidence which the FBI later admitted it had fabricated. This related to testimony from a mentally disturbed Indian woman — that she had seen Leonard Peltier with a gun near the wounded agents' car — which was later shown to have been given under pressure from the FBI. The judge refused to allow her to be called as a defence witness despite the defence lawyers' contention that her testimony was relevant to the credibility of other witnesses against Leonard Peltier. These and other factors have led Amnesty International to conclude that justice would best be served if the US authorities were to grant Leonard Peltier a retrial.

The FBI agents who died in the confrontation had driven onto the reservation to locate four individuals wanted on charges of armed robbery and assault with a deadly weapon. The charges apparently arose from an incident involving the theft of some cowboy boots from two white youths. It has been AIM's contention that the Native Americans' actions, including firing on the agents, were taken in legitimate self-defence. The prosecution maintained, however, that the fact that the two agents were killed at close range invalidated the self-defence argument in Leonard Peltier's case. Two other Native Americans who were accused in connection with the killings were acquitted after their lawyers contended that they apparently could have been acting in self-defence given the atmosphere of fear and violence existing on the reservation.

Leonard Peltier has always denied killing the agents. According to AIM, he had gone to the Pine Ridge Reservation in response to an invitation from "traditionals" (Indians who attempt to follow ancestral spiritual and cultural practices). The Pine Ridge Reservation is rich in uranium deposits reportedly needed for government energy and defence projects, and the official tribal government, said by "traditionals" to have been installed with federal support and approval, was reportedly willing to cooperate with US corporations interested in mining the uranium. The "traditionals" were opposed to this and invited AIM to Pine Ridge in an effort to stop the uranium being mined. They feared the mining would result in toxic waste being dumped on the reservation and scarce water being drained from under it. The "traditionals" also apparently wished to obtain protection from an armed group of civilians allegedly employed by the Pine Ridge tribal government and said to be working with Bureau of Indian Affairs (BIA) police, which the "traditionals" alleged had harassed, beaten and murdered AIM supporters and "traditionals" on the reservation.

The FBI regarded AIM's presence on the reservation as agitation and asserted that AIM members were heavily armed and dug into fortified bunkers. AIM itself maintained that the FBI had initiated a police build-up in the area in response to AIM's presence on the reserve and that this had led the Indians to fear that their lives were in danger. It pointed to several incidents in previous years when massive build-ups of police and military fire-power in response to protests or other incidents involving Native Americans had led to confrontations between the security forces and the Indians, resulting in some cases in Indian deaths.Political opposition to the government or trade union activities have also led to human rights violations against indigenous leaders and activists. In 1981 Aymara peasant leader Genaro Flores was shot and paralysed from the waist down when he was abducted by the Bolivian police. Amnesty International believed he was singled out because of his peaceful trade union activities and sent a delegation to La Paz to press the government to acknowledge his detention. Medical treatment was arranged for him in France after which, although still confined to a wheelchair, Genaro Flores was able to return to Bolivia and resume his leading role in the peasant movement.

In May 1989 Amnesty International expressed concern at reports that exiled members of the Guatemalan opposition, including indigenous leader Rigoberta Menchú, had received death threats after returning to the country to participate in the National Dialogue. Amnesty International called for urgent measures to be taken to protect the delegation, for an immediate investigation into the threats they had received, and for those responsible to be brought to justice. To Amnesty International's knowledge, the death threats against Rigoberto Menchú have not been investigated.

All over the world people, including indigenous people, who take action in response to

Rigoberta Menchú, an internationally-known indigenous leader from Quiché, was forced into exile in the early 1980s, after her father, mother and a brother had been killed by the Guatemalan security forces. When she returned to Guatemala in May 1989 to participate in internal peace talks she received death threats. She is shown here leading the international march for indigenous rights which followed a meeting in Guatemala in October 1991. The meeting was called by indigenous organizations to discuss activities to highlight the plight of indigenous peoples during 1992.

87

human rights violations against their relatives often become some of the leading human rights activists in their countries. These relatives are endlessly in the front line, campaigning for a prisoner's release, confronting government officials, trying to get information, to obtain compensation, or to care for prisoners. As a result they themselves have often become the victims of human rights violations.

Members of CONAVIGUA, the mainly indigenous Guatemalan widows' association, have campaigned for compensation for their husbands' deaths or "disappearances", and have tried to find their "disappeared" relatives or exhume their bodies from clandestine cemeteries. They have also opposed forced recruitment of their sons into the Guatemalan military and the nominally voluntary civil defence patrols. In rural areas of Guatemala, young Indian youths have been forcibly seized, often as they left religious or social gatherings, taken from their local communities to military barracks some distance away, and trained there for military service. Young men of non-indigenous backgrounds are customarily not subjected to such forcible conscription and imposed military service. As a result of campaigning on such issues, CONAVIGUA members have been victims of death threats, arbitrary detentions and assaults by the army, allegedly including rape, apparently intended to deter them from pursuing their aims.

CONAVIGUA member Juana Calachij has reportedly survived three attempts to abduct her by members of the local civil defence patrol. She was singled out because of her campaign for the exhumation of a clandestine grave at Pacoc, El Quiché. The exhumation was conducted in June 1988 and the bodies of her husband and four others killed in 1984 by the civil defence patrol were returned to their families for burial. Amnesty International knows of no efforts to investigate the circumstances of the victims' death. Nor have the attempts to abduct Juana Calachij been investigated. Two of them occurred after the exhumation.

'Don't help the indigenous, don't help the poor'

When US nun Dianna Ortiz went to work in Guatemala in 1989, she particularly asked to work in an indigenous community because "indigenous people have suffered the most". Over the next two years she received a series of death threats, apparently because of her educational work with young indigenous children in

Exhumation of a clandestine grave in Pacoc, El Quiché, Guatemala, in 1988

the largely Chuj community of San Miguel, Huehuetenango. In November 1989 she was abducted by men in plain clothes who turned her over to uniformed police officers driving an official police car. While in their custody, she was tortured, including being subjected to rape and sexual abuse which she later said was "too horrible to describe". A nun who had worked with Sister Dianna said of the San Miguel community that "There's not one single family up there that doesn't have members either 'disappeared' or killed. The fact that Dianna was kidnapped, tortured and raped is unusual only because she's still alive.... I think the message they're sending to the church is clear: Don't help the indigenous, don't help the poor".

In many countries in the Americas, people who work in indigenous communities or support their aims have been singled out for human rights violations.

Aid and medical personnel working in Mexico with Guatemalan refugees, many of the latter indigenous people who fled their homes to escape widespread violations carried out by the Guatemalan army against indigenous communities in their area, have on a number of occasions been subjected to

Luz Estrella Vargas, a religious layworker, "disappeared" in Colombia in 1987 with another layworker and two indigenous leaders. They were on their way to a meeting called to support a local indigenous community threatened with eviction from traditional land. Their bodies were found several days later; all had been shot in the head. Eye-witnesses stated that they had been detained by the police.

violations including torture and extrajudicial execution carried out in Mexico by the Guatemalan army and paramilitary units working with them.

In the USA, Amnesty International adopted as a prisoner of conscience churchworker Stacey Merkt, who was imprisoned in 1987 for transporting and conspiring to transport illegal "aliens". She started serving six months of an 18-month prison sentence in January 1987, while pregnant with her first child, but was released from prison in April to serve the rest of her sentence under house arrest. The "aliens" in question were Central Americans, some of them of indigenous origin, whom Amnesty International believed to be at risk of human rights violations including "disappearance" and extrajudicial execution if returned to their countries of origin. Although Amnesty International did not dispute the right of the USA to enforce its immigration laws, it concluded that Stacey Merkt had been convicted of breaking laws which, in practice, directly facilitated human rights violations to which the organization was opposed.

For many years, those who work in indigenous communities in Peru have been the victims of human rights violations. In 1981 Amnesty International adopted as a prisoner of conscience Nicolás Matayoshi, a poet, novelist and educator, who specialized in preparing educational materials for children speaking only Quechua. He had been arrested as an "intellectual terrorist", whose writings had "encouraged terrorist acts". He was later cleared of all charges.

In Guatemala, a number of indigenous radio presenters have "disappeared" or been killed; they had broadcast educational and self-help programs in indigenous languages. In July 1988 an indigenous priest in El Quiché received death threats after he organized and broadcast a mass for Indian widows in the local indigenous language, Quiché. The mass was attended by some 1,800 people, many of them indigenous women whose husbands had been the victims of army counter-insurgency campaigns in the early 1980s. The priest was forced to abandon his parish and go into hiding. He told Amnesty International: "They say that I am giving orders to the widows, but the law says one has the right to organize. And the most scorned, forgotten people here are women: married women, but especially the Indian widows".

Scores of other victims of "disappearance" and extrajudicial execution in Guatemala over the years appear to have been singled out because they had studied and publicized the desperate situation of Guatemala's Indians. Myrna Mack Chang, a Guatemalan anthropologist of Chinese descent working with indigenous people, had conducted research on a subject considered highly sensitive by the Guatemalan military: the situation of those Guatemalans displaced by the army counter-insurgency campaigns of the late 1970s and early 1980s. She was brutally stabbed to death in September 1990 as she left her office at a social science research institute in Guatemala City. The investigation lasted for more than a year. The police detective investigating the case, José Mérida Escobar, was shot dead on 5 August 1991 as he was preparing to leave the country to testify about the case before the Inter-American Commission on Human Rights. He claimed to have found evidence of the involvement of the military. Journalists and judicial officials working on the case were also intimidated and threatened. The man charged with killing Myrna Mack Chang was arrested in Los Angeles, USA, and is now on trial in Guatemala. A former member of the military Presidential High Command, he had previously worked with the Department of Criminal Investigations (DIC) of the National Police.

Those who have worked with indigenous people have also been victimized by armed opposition groups. In Peru, an Australian nun of the Order of Saint Joseph of the Sacred Heart, Irene McCormack, was publicly executed in May 1991 by the PCP. She was killed with a number of local community officials after a mock trial in the main square of Huasahuasi, a small community in the central Andean highlands. Sister Irene had taught reading, games and liturgy to impoverished children and young people in the heavily indigenous department of Junín, where she died. According to witnesses, members of the PCP accused her of being "an American Yankee". Local people said that the PCP sees the church as a threat to its political influence.

'We want respect for our rights'

There are at least nine million indigenous people in Mexico out of a total population of over 80 million, according to the most recent census, making up 56 ethnic groups living mainly in rural areas in the central and southern regions. Many of Mexico's indigenous people belong to the poorest sectors of the population; historically they have been victims of "disappearance", extrajudicial execution, torture and arbitrary detention. In recent years a growing number of independent organizations have been formed to campaign for indigenous rights by pressing claims to land and challenging a perceived lack of democracy in municipal and community affairs. One of these organizations, the Movement for Triqui Unity and Struggle (MULT), was founded in 1981 to secure the claims of the Triqui Indians of western Oaxaca to disputed woodlands and communal land. MULT members and leaders have since suffered numerous abuses.

Ecuador is estimated to have one of the largest indigenous populations in the Americas. They live throughout the country, on the Pacific Coast, in the Amazon basin and in the highlands, where most subsist by eking out a living on small plots of land. Increased pressure on land, attributed by indigenous groups to the activities of petroleum companies, settlers, missionaries and tourist development, as well as population growth, united many Ecuadorian indigenous groups in an Indian protest movement in June 1990. Led by the Confederation of Indigenous Nationalities of Ecuador (CONAIE), Indians blocked access to highland provinces, occupied public buildings and cut off food supplies to towns. They demanded a solution to land issues, particularly disputes involving highland Indians which they felt had largely been ignored by the Ecuadorian authorities or had stalled in the courts. Other demands included indigenous peoples' "inalienable rights to self determination"; reform of the Constitution to acknowledge Ecuador as a multi-national state; the recuperation and communal possession of indigenous ancestral territories; adoption of Quechua as an official language alongside Spanish; basic infrastructure for Indian communities; and the expulsion of the US-based Summer Institute of Linguistics (SIL) missionary group. Ecuadorian indigenous groups have complained that SIL has shown a lack of respect for Indian cultures and had pursued policies of resettlement that had contributed to epidemics which had taken the lives of many Indians.

Following the protest, the government agreed to participate in a dialogue with indigenous groups. However, indigenous communities have complained that the dialogue has been ineffective, particularly in relation to land disputes which have resulted in the expulsion of Indian communities from their lands, and harassment, torture and killings.In April 1992 CONAIE once again led a major action by Ecuadorian Indian communities. Quechuas, Shiwiars, Achuars and Záperos marched from the Amazon region of Ecuador to the capital, Quito, to present a series of demands to the government. They asked among other things for decision-making power over petroleum exploration on their traditional lands. Initially, Ecuadorian President Rodrigo Borja Cevallos said his government would grant land to the Indians, but negotiations stalled when the army accused the Indians of trying to create a parallel state and announced that it would refuse to recognize any claims to territory within 50 kilometres of the border with Peru.

Some three million Quechua and one million Aymara-speaking people inhabit the highlands of Bolivia; between 150,000 and 200,000 others, representing 30 indigenous groups, live in the lowlands. Many joined a 400-mile "March for Dignity" in 1990, organized to protest that despite a government plan for the conservation of traditional indigenous areas in Bolivia's eastern lowlands, colonists and cattle ranchers had moved onto the land and timbering companies were openly operating there. The march received

A section of the "March for dignity", organized by indigenous groups in Bolivia. The banner reads: "For our land and our dignity". The 400-mile march took place in 1990 to protest against encroachments on traditional indigenous lands.

widespread national and international attention; President Jaime Paz Zamora and most of his cabinet travelled to meet the Indians half-way to the capital, La Paz, and promised to establish a commission to demarcate the disputed lands. However, indigenous people have complained that ranchers who had moved on to their lands have not been removed.

In Guatemala, the Council of Ethnic Communities "Runujel Junam" (CERJ) was formed in 1988 to struggle for indigenous rights. One of the key issues in their campaign is to secure the constitutionally guaranteed right not to serve in the military-imposed civil defence patrols. CERJ members have repeatedly been characterized as "subversives" by the authorities and subjected to human rights violations. Between 1988 and 1992 Amnesty International recorded a series of abuses against CERJ members including seven "disappearances" and at least 13 apparent extrajudicial executions. Some of the abuses were carried out by military personnel, either in uniform or plain clothes, others by unidentified heavily armed men believed to be acting under military orders.

Indigenous peoples in Colombia, where the Indian population is estimated at 450,000, are also organizing to defend their rights, traditions, and religions. The National Indigenous Organization of Colombia (ONIC) is one of several groups working at the national level to defend indigenous interests. In the Cauca area, the CRIC has been struggling to recover traditional territories and to defend the rights of indigenous peoples in the fertile Cauca River valley. They have recently appealed to the government for protection against drug traffickers in the area, reportedly without success.

In the USA, an important catalyst to indigenous activism were the so-called "fishing rights cases". These disputes arose from conflicts between indigenous customary law and practice and certain fishing rights formally granted Indian groups by treaty, and national or state laws. The National Indian Youth Council formed in the USA in 1960 has been active in organizing Indians all over the country to protest the arrest and convictions of Indians who attempted to exercise fishing rights which they say were guaranteed them in treaties. Other disputes on which North American Indian groups were active concerned groups which live on either side of and do not recognize the US-Canada border, who have been prosecuted for trading or carrying dutiable items across the border. In some cases, their territorial boundaries straddling the border were recognized or guaranteed in treaties. Other North American indigenous groups direct their attention specifically to educational or legal programs intended to benefit Native Americans. The Native American Rights Fund, for example, encourages Indian groups not recognized as such by the US Government to present claims to have their traditional lands returned to them.

These organizations and their activities are but a small sample of recent developments in the struggle for indigenous rights.

Recently coordination between indigenous groups has been strengthened by the national and regional meetings held throughout the Americas to plan activities highlighting the plight of indigenous peoples during 1992.

Indigenous people are also pressing their demands with increasing vigour at the international level. In recent years, a number of sub-regional, regional and international gatherings of indigenous people have been held, and a number of indigenous organizations have been formed at sub-regional, regional and international level. The Inuit Circumpolar Conference, for example, works on behalf of Inuits, including those resident in the Americas, while the International Indian Treaty Council, which seeks wider knowledge of and respect for treaties signed between Indian nations and countries, brings together various indigenous organizations from the USA and Canada. Other regional organizations include the Regional Council of Indigenous Peoples of Central America, Mexico and Panama and the Indigenous Council of South America. Other organizations bring together indigenous parliamentarians, jurists, journalists, writers and women.

At an international level, the World Council of Indigenous Peoples had its genesis in a conference of indigenous peoples held in British Columbia, Canada, in 1975 and has since drawn up declarations of principles on the rights of indigenous peoples. Several hundred indigenous groups and individuals now place their concerns before the annual session of the UN Working Group on Indigenous Populations.

"What we want is respect for our rights ...We are worried because the non-Indians think that we are a different race. Therefore, they want to isolate us ... They do not worry very much about what is going on with us ... But you should pressure the Brazilian Government and every government in the world because they are all alike ... I want you to do something — something real to help the Indians ... We need to survive." With this statement, delivered to the IACHR in September 1990, Yanomami leader Davi Kopenawa Yanomami focused international attention on the plight of his indigenous community.

The Yanomami, estimated in 1988 to number 9,000, are the largest of Brazil's indigenous groups to have maintained their traditional way of life, largely due to their previous isolation. Their traditional lands lie in the remote rainforest straddling the border between Brazil and Venezuela.

Since the 1970s the Yanomami have suffered major incursion onto their lands, as a result of government projects which stimulated exploration and settlement of indigenous areas. After 1973 the government's Program of National Integration brought settlers, road construction gangs and gold prospectors into the region. A new gold rush began in 1987 after the military-inspired *Calha Norte* project encouraged colonization along Brazil's 6,500 kilometre border with Colombia, Venezuela, Guyana, Suriname and French Guiana. After 1987, reports of violent attacks on the Yanomami by armed miners increased; attacks which the government did little to prevent and less to punish. Following a clash between the Yanomami and armed gold prospectors in 1987 in which four Indians died, FUNAI prohibited the entry of missionaries and anthropologists where the incident had occurred, making it difficult to investigate. The forcible removal from the area of Italian missionaries who had been providing the Yanomami with health care, also led to an increased rate of fatalities from infectious diseases and mercury poisoning among the Yanomami. The diseases, to which the Indians had no immunity, had been introduced by the prospectors; the mercury pollution is the result of mining techniques.

There was widespread national and international support for the Yanomami and pressure on the government to protect them. UN Secretary-General Javier Pérez de Cuéllar wrote to Brazilian President Fernando Collor, and the IACHR and numerous non-governmental organizations made representations to the government. A law suit was filed in Brazil on behalf of the Yanomami by Survival International, an independent group which campaigns for the rights of indigenous peoples throughout the world. In a statement before the IACHR representative of the US-based Indian Law Resource Centre, who had conducted research in Yanomami territory in 1990, declared that the number of gold miners, their wealth, and their militancy, had enabled them to control local officials and block federal efforts to secure Yanomami lands.

As a result, steps were taken to demarcate Yanomami lands. From January 1990 Brazil's federal police conducted several operations to remove miners from Yanomami territory. In November 1991 the government announced that it intended to set aside 23 million acres for the Yanomami. The area was formally demarcated in May 1992.

However, new incursions by gold miners into Yanomami lands have been reported recently. In addition, many of those expelled moved onto the traditional lands of the neighbouring Macuxí Indians, who were increasingly the victims of violent attack. In February 1992 the government banned journalists and researchers from the Yanomami area.

5

Conclusions and proposals

Conclusions

Indigenous peoples in the Americas continue to be deprived of internationally recognized human rights: civil and political rights as well as economic, social and cultural rights. Deprivation and discrimination in areas such as health care, education, housing and land have been documented by others. In Amnesty International's area of expertise it has documented in this report and elsewhere gross and persistent human rights violations against indigenous peoples of the Americas including extrajudicial execution and the judicial death penalty, "disappearance", torture and ill-treatment (including rape and sexual abuse), unfair trial, and imprisonment as prisoners of conscience. The discrimination and economic deprivation which indigenous peoples suffer can render them particularly vulnerable to the human rights abuses Amnesty International works against; some sectors, such as refugees, displaced people and isolated groups, can be more vulnerable still.

No one is safe: the victims have included indigenous political, religious, and community leaders, women, children and old people. Those who work with indigenous peoples or support their cause, relatives of indigenous activists and those who have witnessed abuses have also become the victims of human rights violations.

Indigenous peoples suffer these violations for a variety of reasons. They may be singled out because of their ethnic or national origins or because they are outspoken activists on behalf of indigenous rights. In situations of internal conflict, indigenous people resident in contested areas may be subjected to abuses by both sides.

In other contexts, simply to be resident in areas where official security agents are engaged in anti-drugs operations, or where governments favour non-indigenous settlement in order to secure frontiers for reasons of "national security" may render indigenous people vulnerable to abuses.

Many violations directed against indigenous peoples stem from the struggle for land and resources; often their lands and resources, or lands and resources they claim, may be wanted by the state or commercial interests for economic exploitation. In such contexts, indigenous peoples may become vulnerable to abuses by state agents, or may find that the state does not investigate or prosecute effectively abuses carried out by non-state agents.

The discrimination and social and economic deprivation which many indigenous peoples suffer means they often have limited or no access to adequate legal representation, and makes it more difficult for them to seek redress when their rights are violated.

Members of the security forces have been named as responsible for human rights violations against indigenous peoples throughout the Americas. These violations have occurred in countries which have legal systems formally protective of the human rights of indigenous peoples. In some contexts, police officers and members of the armed forces have carried out abuses against indigenous peoples in the guise of so-called "death squads". Civil defence squads, formed at military behest and acting under military orders, have also been responsible for human rights violations against indigenous peoples. In some countries, the authorities have colluded or acquiesced in abuses carried out against indigenous peoples by private individuals, including hired gunmen.

In many countries of the Americas, those responsible for abuses, whether state or private agents, appear to benefit from virtual impunity for their deeds.

Throughout the Americas, there has been a resurgence of indigenous organization: groups have been formed at community, national, regional and international level to protect their rights and to bring their demands to public attention. A growing international awareness of environmental and ecological issues coincides in some cases with indigenous peoples' traditional beliefs and practices concerning protection of the environment and has gained indigenous organizations new allies at the international level. Some governments and intergovernmental bodies

©Jenny Matthews

In most parts of the Americas members of the security forces and their civilian auxiliaries have been responsible for human rights violations against indigenous peoples. In several countries in the region, private agents — hired gunmen, civilian vigilantes, armed groups of settlers, drug traffickers — are also responsible for persistent abuses such as the abduction and murder of Indians. These otherwise common crimes become human rights violations when they are committed with official collusion or acquiescence, for example, when the state consistently fails to investigate them or to bring those responsible to justice.

101

are in turn devoting increased attention to the demands and needs of indigenous peoples.

Although much has been accomplished, principally by indigenous peoples themselves, the human rights of indigenous peoples in the Americas continue to be massively abused, and much remains to be done at national and international level to redress the situation.

Recommendations to protect human rights

Many of the abuses suffered by indigenous peoples in the Americas fall outside of the areas of Amnesty International's expertise. Therefore, these recommendations do not directly address important issues such as the provision of health care and education, and other economic, social and cultural rights of indigenous peoples in the region; they are intended to protect those rights on which Amnesty International's mandate focuses.

These recommendations fall into two sections. The first section details protective measures designed to address the special circumstances of indigenous peoples. The second section contains measures which, if enforced, would protect everyone against human rights violations, whether or not they are of indigenous origin.

Section I: Specific protection for indigenous people

Protection of indigenous peoples' rights

1.   Both national and international standards with respect to protection of basic human rights should be enforced in a way which ensures that indigenous peoples enjoy full protection of such rights.

2.   The responsible authorities at all levels — local, state or provincial, federal or central — should ensure that indigenous peoples are effectively protected against human rights abuses.

3.   Effective mechanisms for identifying human rights abuses against indigenous peoples should be put in place, and thorough and impartial investigations should be conducted into all reports of such abuses in order to make the full truth known and bring the perpetrators to justice.

4.   Governments should ensure that any private bodies,

such as commercial enterprises or missionary groups, which have contact with indigenous peoples fully respect the fundamental human rights of indigenous peoples. If abuses do occur, governments should ensure that they are promptly investigated and the perpetrators brought to justice.

5. Legal proceedings against indigenous peoples should always be conducted in their own language or adequate interpretation provided.

6. Since indigenous peoples often do not have access to or the resources to retain legal counsel, to be present at legal proceedings or to ensure the presence of witnesses in their favour, special efforts should be made to ensure full respect for Article 14 of the International Covenant on Civil and Political Rights (ICCPR), including the stipulation that everyone charged with a criminal offence shall have the right to "be tried in his presence, and to defend himself in person or through legal assistance of his own choosing, to be informed if he does not have legal assistance, of this right, and to have legal assistance assigned to him, in any case where the interests of justice so require, and without payment by him in any such case, if he does not have sufficient means to pay for it".

7. Governments should ensure that justice is equally available to all those living within their national borders irrespective of their ethnic origin or the remoteness of the areas in which they live.

8. As newly contacted or isolated indigenous groups are particularly vulnerable, special care must be taken to protect them against human rights abuses.

Land and resource disputes

1. Governments should take account of the principle reflected in Article 18 of the ILO Indigenous and Tribal Peoples Convention No. 169 (1989) as an important factor in efforts to prevent abuses against indigenous peoples in the context of land or resource disputes: "Adequate penalties shall be established by law for unauthorized intrusion upon, or use of, the lands of the peoples concerned, and governments shall take measures to prevent such offences".

2.   Speedy and just resolution of unresolved land conflicts, including those subject to litigation, could also have an impact on reducing the instances of abuses against indigenous peasants which have occurred in many areas of the Americas, often perpetrated by gunmen acting on behalf of state or private interests in the context of land disputes.

3.   Since many abuses against indigenous peoples occur during evictions, steps should be taken to ensure that evictions are not authorized and do not take place except in accordance with fundamental principles of justice and relevant international standards, and taking full account of treaties and laws protecting the lands of indigenous peoples. When evictions do take place, measures should be taken to avoid the use of force and prevent abuses against indigenous peoples. Those occupying the contested land should be adequately informed about relevant court orders before any eviction takes place, and their opportunity to challenge the legality of the eviction order should be ensured. A competent judicial official should accompany police officers empowered to carry out the order. Police officers who carry out authorised evictions should be trained in and obliged to comply with international standards regarding the use of force by law enforcement officers, including the UN Basic Principles on the Use of Force and Firearms by Law Enforcement Officials.

Treatment in prison

The appropriate authorities should review arrangements for the treatment and custody of all prisoners, to ensure that they are treated humanely and in conformity with the UN Body of Principles for the Protection of All Persons under Any Form of Detention or Imprisonment, the UN Standard Minimum Rules for the Treatment of Prisoners, and Article 10 of the ICCPR, which states: "All persons deprived of their liberty shall be treated with humanity and with respect for the inherent dignity of the human person".

- These authorities should take into account the special circumstances and needs of indigenous detainees, including those who may have never before lived apart from their community. They should be detained as near as possible to their community in order to facilitate visits by their relatives, friends, and other community members.

- In situations where there is hostility or racial prejudice against indigenous detainees, whether from guards or other inmates, the authorities should take special steps to protect indigenous detainees.

- The following are among those stipulations of the Standard Minimum Rules which often appear to be breached with respect to indigenous prisoners: Article 41 (3) "Access to a qualified representative of any religion shall not be refused to any prisoner"; Article 42 "So far as is practicable, every prisoner shall be allowed to satisfy the needs of his religious life by attending the services provided in the institution and having in his possession the books of religious observance and instruction of his denomination"; Article 51 (2) "Wherever necessary, the services of an interpreter shall be used".

Discrimination

Governments should recognize that discrimination against indigenous people and other groups is a key contributory factor to human rights abuses, including arbitrary arrest, unfair trial, torture, ill-treatment and summary killing. Governments should initiate a plan of action against such discrimination.

For example, in situations where it is alleged that discrimination in the administration of justice contributes to human rights violations against indigenous peoples — through discriminatory practices in policing, disproportionate prosecution and sentencing, discriminatory treatment in prison, or failure to promptly and thoroughly investigate abuses against indigenous peoples — an independent commission should be established to undertake an impartial inquiry into these allegations and to make recommendations as to how to rectify the situation. Such a commission should carry out its work in close consultation with indigenous and other affected groups.

Human rights monitoring

1. During 1993, the UN International Year for the World's Indigenous People, each government of a country in the Americas where

indigenous peoples reside should initiate a national review, to be carried out by an independent commission or task force, of the extent to which international human rights standards which protect indigenous peoples' rights have been implemented in practice. The rights examined should include all fundamental civil, political, economic, social and cultural rights set forth in the Universal Declaration of Human Rights, the ICCPR and the International Covenant on Economic, Social and Cultural Rights. The review should examine any factors or difficulties which have impeded full compliance with these international human rights standards and recommend steps aimed at ensuring full implementation of indigenous peoples' rights. The review should involve the active participation of representatives of indigenous groups and non-governmental organizations working on behalf of indigenous peoples.

2. In countries where indigenous peoples reside, special efforts should be made by bodies which are charged with investigating reports of human rights violations to monitor the human rights situations in remote parts of the country where indigenous peoples may be the victims of unreported violations. In all cases, efforts should be made to ensure that it is possible to communicate with indigenous peoples in their own languages, or that adequate interpretation is provided so that indigenous people may make known abuses they have suffered.

3. Intergovernmental bodies such as the UN Commission on Human Rights and the Inter-American Commission on Human Rights should ensure that the special situations facing indigenous peoples and the human rights violations they suffer are adequately addressed where relevant in country, thematic and general reporting.

4. The UN Working Group on Indigenous Populations has provided a useful forum for indigenous peoples to draw attention to abuses they have suffered and suggest measures to prevent these abuses. Governments should support efforts by the UN Working Group on Indigenous Populations to promote better protection of the fundamental, internationally-recognized human rights of

indigenous peoples. Governments should be responsive to the Working Group's requests for information and on-site visits, and should take full account of its conclusions, recommendations and proposals aimed at protecting the rights of indigenous peoples and ending human rights violations against them. The member states of the UN should ensure that the Working Group is adequately funded to carry out its important tasks, and that the UN's Voluntary Fund for Indigenous Populations is adequately supported in order that it can carry out its task of facilitating widespread participation of indigenous representatives in the deliberations of the Working Group.

5. The OAS should examine whether indigenous rights are adequately addressed by existing human rights bodies within the inter-American system, and should consider ways of developing more effective protection by regional bodies.

Bilateral and multilateral lending and assistance programs
Governments should ensure that bilateral and multilateral development lending programs with which they are involved take due consideration of the welfare of indigenous people and should make efforts, in consultation with relevant indigenous groups where possible, to ensure that fundamental human rights, including the rights to life and physical integrity, are effectively protected in the course of all development projects, including debt-for-nature swaps.

Human rights awareness
Governments and intergovernmental organizations should make human rights education materials available in indigenous languages and should ensure that indigenous peoples are aware of their rights, and know how to seek redress if their rights are violated.

Abuses during armed conflict
In the context of armed conflict, indigenous peoples in the Americas have often been among the victims of abuses not only by government forces but also by armed opposition groups. Amnesty International reiterates its call on all sides to such conflicts to stop the torture and killing of prisoners, other deliberate and arbitrary killings, and hostage-taking. These abuses are

contrary to the most basic principles of humane conduct derived from international humanitarian law as laid down in Common Article 3 of the Geneva Conventions.

Section II: Measures to protect everyone's human rights

Prevention of abuses

1. No exceptional circumstances whatsoever, whether a state of war or threat or war, internal political instability, or any other public emergency, may be invoked as a justification for torture, "disappearance" or extrajudicial execution. Clear orders should be issued to all security forces and their auxiliaries, such as civil defence patrols and civilian militias, that they must act within the framework of national and international law and that they must cooperate fully with the investigation of human rights violations.

2. All members of the security forces and their auxiliaries should be instructed that they have a duty not to obey orders which will result in human rights violations, and reminded that under international standards obedience to superior orders cannot be considered a defence against accusations of human rights violations.

3. Specific measures should be taken to prevent extrajudicial execution, "disappearance" and torture.

    - Governments should ensure strict control, including a clear chain of command, over all officials responsible for arrest, detention and imprisonment.

    - Effective protection should be guaranteed to individuals and groups who are in danger of extrajudicial executions, including those who receive death threats.

    - All security forces should keep records of the identities of those agents who participated in arrest, detention and interrogation of detainees and, in situations of internal conflict, of officers and soldiers deployed on counter-insurgency patrols.

    - Governments should establish rules setting forth which judicial or other officials are authorized to order detentions.

Arrest, interrogation and detention must be carried out only by officials who are authorized to do so.

● All detainees should be held in officially recognized places of detention. Accurate information on their custody and whereabouts, including transfers, should be made promptly available to their relatives and lawyers.

● Any form of detention or imprisonment and all measures affecting the human rights of detainees should be subject to the effective control of a judicial authority.

● All detainees should be brought promptly before a judge, and given prompt and regular access to lawyers, relatives and doctors. There should be regular independent visits of inspection to places of detention.

● Statements obtained from detainees as a result of torture should never be admissible in legal proceedings, except against the perpetrators.

● International humanitarian organizations which monitor the conditions of political detainees should be granted unrestricted access to all places where such detainees are held.

Investigation of abuses

1. All reports of human rights abuses should be promptly, thoroughly and impartially investigated. The full truth about the abuses should be made known and those responsible brought to justice. Adequate funds and personnel should be allocated to ensure that this occurs, no matter how remote the area where the abuse reportedly occurred. In cases of "disappearance", the investigation should not be curtailed as long as the fate of the victim remains unknown. No impunity for abuses, in law or in practice, should be permitted. Collusion between law enforcement officials and private parties in instigating or perpetrating abuses should be fully investigated.

2. Governments should ensure that all necessary measures are taken to protect victims and witnesses who wish to give evidence of human rights violations, as well as journalists and human rights monitors investigating such abuses.

3. Prosecutors investigating reported abuses should have access to all military and police installations where detainees are believed to be held, and access to all records relating to arrest, detention and interrogation. Obstruction of investigations into human rights violations should be strictly sanctioned.

4. In those countries in the Americas where clandestine cemeteries are known or alleged to exist, the governments concerned should arrange for exhumations. The remains of people buried in these graves should be subjected to proper forensic examination, in order to identify the victims, determine how they died, and who was responsible. The remains of the victims should be returned to their families for proper burial.

The death penalty

1. All governments in the Americas whose laws provide for the death penalty should abolish this cruel, inhuman and degrading punishment. Until the death penalty has been abolished in law throughout the Americas, there should be a moratorium on executions, all death sentences should be commuted, and no death sentences imposed.

2. In countries where the death penalty is imposed a commission of inquiry should be conducted into the effect of racial discrimination and other adverse factors, such as economic and social deprivation, on the application of the death penalty.

Protection of women in detention

To reduce the risk of rape and other sexual abuse, women prisoners should be held separately from male prisoners, and under the supervision of female guards. Measures should be taken to ensure that imprisoned women, particularly those who are pregnant, have recently given birth, or who state that they were subjected to rape or other sexual abuse during arrest or interrogation, are provided with adequate medical care.

Refugees and internally displaced people

1. No one should be forcibly returned to a country where he or she risks imprisonment as a prisoner of conscience, torture, "disappearance" or extrajudicial execution.

Governments should provide such people with effective and durable protection against return.

2. In situations where refugees are in danger of human rights violations in their place of exile, whether carried out by agents from their own country or of the state where they have sought refuge, governments should take steps to ensure refugees' security.

3. The fundamental human rights of the internally displaced must be respected, and the primary duty lies with governments. However, in situations where governments have shown a disregard for the human rights of the displaced, and especially when the displaced are viewed with suspicion by governments engaged in internal armed conflicts, the international community should undertake effective action to offer the displaced the protection they have been denied by their own government and to which they would be entitled were they to cross an international border.

Compensation

Victims of human rights abuses, or their families in cases of extrajudicial execution and "disappearance", should receive compensation for the human rights violations they have suffered. This should include medical treatment and rehabilitation where necessary, and financial compensation commensurate with the abuses inflicted.

Human rights education

Governments should ensure that all law enforcement agents and members of the armed forces receive adequate training on national and international human rights standards and how to enforce them properly.

International human rights standards

All governments should protect the basic human rights guaranteed by the Universal Declaration of Human Rights, including those within the scope of Amnesty International's mandate, such as the rights to life, physical integrity, fair trial and equality before the law, freedom from arbitrary arrest, freedom of conscience, religion, expression, association and assembly. Governments are obliged to ensure that these and other rights are upheld without distinction of any kind, such as race, colour, sex, language, religion, political or other opinion, property, birth or other status.

International instruments which provide more specificity to rights outlined in the Universal Declaration of Human Rights, include: the International Covenant on Civil and Political Rights; the International Covenant on Economic, Social and Cultural Rights; the Convention on the Elimination of All Forms of Racial Discrimination; the Convention against Torture and Other Cruel, Inhuman or Degrading Treatment or Punishment; the Convention on the Prevention and Punishment of the Crime of Genocide; the Convention on the Elimination of All Forms of Discrimination against Women, the Convention on the Rights of the Child; the Convention and Protocol relating to the Status of Refugees; the American Declaration on the Rights and Duties of Man; the American Convention on Human Rights; and the ILO Convention on Indigenous and Tribal Peoples (No. 169).

ENDNOTES

Introduction

[1] In Latin American countries, a *ladino* can be a non-indigenous person or a mixed race person, or one who no longer maintains indigenous customs and practices.

Chapter 1

[2] The whole range of rights set out in international human rights instruments are applicable to indigenous communities. Relevant instruments include:

— the Universal Declaration of Human Rights;
— the International Covenant on Civil and Political Rights;
— the International Covenant on Economic, Social and Cultural Rights;
— the International Convention on the Elimination of All Forms of Racial Discrimination;
— the Convention against Torture and Other Cruel, Inhuman or Degrading Treatment or Punishment;
— the Convention on the Prevention and Punishment of the Crime of Genocide;
— the Convention on the Elimination of All Forms of Discrimination against Women;
— the Convention on the Rights of the Child;
— the Convention and Protocol relating to the Status of Refugees;
— the American Declaration of the Rights and Duties of Man;
— the American Convention on Human Rights.

Chapter 3

[3] Human Rights *Fact Sheet* No 5, published by the Centre for Human Rights, United Nations Office at Geneva.

[4] Part I of the Constitution Act 1982

APPENDIX

Indigenous peoples — towards a definition

An estimated 30 million indigenous people live in the Americas today, the descendants of the pre-Colombian peoples who were once the region's only inhabitants. Defining concepts such as tribal or indigenous lies outside Amnesty International's competence. This is a complex area which has long been the subject of debate and discussion among jurists, academics, international organizations and indigenous peoples themselves. However, in its work on indigenous peoples Amnesty International takes account of the definition adopted by the International Labour Organization (ILO) in its Indigenous and Tribal Peoples Convention of 1989. The ILO's definition appears to be increasingly referred to by those working in the field as at least a working definition, while others, such as the UN Working Group on Indigenous Populations, are developing their own definitions.

The ILO Convention applies to two categories of people: "tribal peoples in independent countries whose social, cultural and economic conditions distinguish them from other sections of the national community, and whose status is regulated wholly or partially by their own customs or traditions or by special laws or regulations"; and "peoples in independent countries who are regarded as indigenous on account of their descent from the populations which inhabited the country, or a geographical region to which the country belongs, at the time of conquest or colonisation or the establishment of present state boundaries and who, irrespective of their legal status, retain some or all of their own social, economic, cultural and political institutions".

The Convention also states that "self-identification as indigenous or tribal shall be regarded as a fundamental criterion for determining the groups to which the provisions of this convention apply"